MY WORLD

PETER SAGAN

with John Deering

MY WORLD

Boulder, Colorado

4745 Walnut Street, Unit A
Boulder, CO 80301–2587 USA

VeloPress is the leading publisher of books on endurance sports and is a division
of Pocket Outdoor Media. Focused on cycling, triathlon, running, swimming,
and nutrition/diet, VeloPress books help athletes achieve their goals of going
faster and farther. Preview books and contact us at velopress.com.

Distributed in the United States and Canada by Ingram Publisher Services

ISBN 9781948007122 (paperback)
The Library of Congress has cataloged the hardcover edition as follows:

Names: Sagan, Peter, 1990- author. | Deering, John, author.
Title: My world / Peter Sagan ; with John Deering.
Description: Boulder, CO : VeloPress, 2018. | Includes index. |
Identifiers: LCCN 2018045051 (print) | LCCN 2018046888 (ebook) |
ISBN 9781948006118 (ebook) | ISBN 9781937715946 (hardcover)
Subjects: LCSH: Sagan, Peter, 1990- | Cyclists--Slovakia--Biography.
Classification: LCC GV1051.S33 (ebook) | LCC GV1051.S33 A3 2018 (print) |
DDC 796.6/2092 [B] --dc23
LC record available at https://lccn.loc.gov/2018045051

This paper meets the requirements of ANSI/NISO Z39.48-1992 (Permanence of Paper).

19 20 21 / 10 9 8 7 6 5 4 3 2 1

To my son, Marlon.

This book is about my biggest victories in cycling.

You are my biggest victory in life.

CONTENTS

PROLOGUE

For the 10th time today, the masts of the tall ships loom up on our right. The scent in my nostrils changes as it always does at this point. From the damp cool of a Scandinavian weekend afternoon to the tang of the harbor, flavored with the smoky promise of dozens of fast-food grills selling every kind of edible meat or fish that you can cram into some bread and sell to a hungry cycling fan.

This is the long sweeping left-hand bend that separates the waterfront from the colorful townhouses that characterize this beautiful old port. The first time we came along here, it was at quite a gentle pace, with barely 40 kilometers ridden. That must have been shortly after 11:00 a.m. this morning. The next half a dozen or so times we came past those rocking masts and chattering rigging, the intensity had risen enough to mean there were fewer cyclists hanging on each time. There were nearly 200 of us this morning; now, after the last two or three hard laps of this hilly little circuit in Bergen, there look to be around 60 of us left. A Union Cycliste Internationale (UCI) official starts clanging furiously at a big old brass bell to tell us that there is one lap to go. I'm suddenly acutely aware of the No. 1 on my back. It's now four in the afternoon, and I've probably got about half an hour left as UCI World Champion.

The race was really confusing.

It had started slow, which suited me. I hadn't eaten or drunk properly for a couple of days since having a ridiculously badly timed upset stomach at home in Monaco on Friday. And that had followed a week off the bike due to a flu virus. I don't want to moan about being sick because it doesn't happen that often, but suffice it to say the last month was not the preparation I'd had in mind going into one of the highlight events of the racing calendar. I'd been world champion for the past two years, and there was every chance that I was going to lose the UCI rainbow jersey today even if I'd been in splendid health. Most people were predicting that the circuit would be too difficult for a rider they considered to be a "sprinter who could get over a hill" rather than a true *puncheur* like Julian Alaphilippe, Philippe Gilbert, or my predecessor as world champion, Michal Kwiatkowski (or Kwiato, as we call him). They also thought that I would be too well marked to succeed a third time, with the bigger teams whistling "Won't Get Fooled Again" to themselves. In addition, the smart money believed that those same teams would swamp our little Slovakian band of brothers when we needed to control the race.

A break had gone away early. The race began in a little town not far away before settling into these dozen circuits of downtown Bergen, the harborside, the seafront, Salmon Hill. So many races go through a desperate scramble in the first hour as everybody tries to get themselves into the day-long race-shaping break that will inevitably be hauled back by the strongest riders, but fortunately for my churning stomach that never happened. The break formed. It went. By the time they were 10 minutes up the road, the rest of us 200 or so hopefuls started riding a bit, and by then I was beginning to feel like a bike rider again.

I should have been here for the last 10 days or so. I had been planning to hook up with my BORA-hansgrohe teammates for the team time trial a week before today. The TTT is a relatively new addition to the world cycling championships roster, and it's a bit weird as you still ride for your regular professional team, rather than your country, as in every other event at the world's. That opportunity to wave a patriotic flag rather than wear the baseball cap of a bank, bike company, or a kitchen exhaust fan manufacturer is what gives the world's such a draw for fans. Also, as the racing takes place over a circuit rather than point-to-point, it's a much more watchable event for the fans, and they come from all over the world to shout, cheer, drink, and—hopefully—celebrate. Slovakians are very good at all these testing disciplines.

BORA-hansgrohe had claimed a top-ten finish in my absence, and my Slovakian teammates were expecting to be doing the road race without me too. I'd hauled my sorry, sweaty ass out of bed and flown out of Nice yesterday morning, spending most of the 2,500 kilometers in the toilet.

I'd been pretty quiet on the start line, glad, and, frankly, amazed just to be there. As we passed over the finish line for the first time when we reached the Bergen circuit, I turned to my brother Juraj riding alongside me, both of us resplendent in our blue, red, and white Slovakia skinsuits. "Take a good look," I told him. "I don't think we'll be seeing this line again."

But the steady pace was good for me, and so was the mild temperature. A year ago, I'd won this title in searing heat in Qatar. I couldn't see my dehydrated body getting away with that again; Norway was a lot more accommodating.

I buried myself in the heart of the bunch. It was decreasing in numbers gradually as the race went on. The world's always has a high dropout rate for a number of reasons. One: A lot of nations send riders to make up the numbers to keep their foot in the door with the powers that be and try to ensure they don't lose those places in subsequent years. Two: Many riders are there to control, chase, or get in breaks in the first half of the race for their team leaders, and their jobs are complete before the real action begins. Three: It's a really, really long race—267 kilometers in 2017—at the end of a long season, and you have to ride past the welcoming, warm, dry pit area many times. You can feel your handlebars begin to turn in of their own accord, the magnetic pull increasing with each lap. You might even be able to see your hotel from the route.

It was fairly steady until about five laps to go. Then the Dutch guys all got on the front, and everything became distinctly uncomfortable. The Netherlands always seem to bring seemingly unending numbers of powerful horses to the world's, and if you're in the bunch and you see what seems like dozens of 80-kilogram six-foot-plus musclemen in orange jerseys get on the front, it's always time to take a deep breath and grit your teeth. The "fasten seatbelts" sign goes on in your head. You know it's going to get bumpy.

Paradoxically, nobody from Holland has won this race in my lifetime. But while they might not have been kings for a long time, they have the ability to be kingmakers, inadvertently or not.

I'd been through a few tests by this time, and mentally I counted them off. Test one: Get to Bergen. Tick. Test two: Start race. Tick. Test three: Look like a cyclist for an hour. Tick.

This was test four: Survive an injection of pace. Oh well, I'll never be one to die wondering. Better get on with it, Peter.

―――――――

There were about a hundred of us left. After a race is over, I am often asked to explain how it unfolded, especially if I've won, as if it were a novel I'd written, shuffling characters around, plotting the action, throwing in a few red herrings, and placing the hero in peril. It's an attractive conceit, and I can see why they would like me to take up the invitation, but it's not possible. They're not wrong that there is a narrative, but it's just my narrative. There are a hundred guys each with a story, each story different to everybody else's. I can only tell mine. You know GoPro cameras? They're great, eh? One fixed to the front of a bike can give you real excitement and a feel for the internal workings of a race. Now imagine that was your *only* view of the race. The world championships in Bergen without helicopter coverage, without motorcycle coverage, without finish-line cameras, without commentary, all six and a half hours of it. Well, that's my story, my movie, my narrow version of the hundred versions, and I don't think we'd find many willing viewers for that.

I hung on. Focused on the wheel in front. Hid, really. I'm used to riding near the front to see what's going on, and it turns out that it's all a bit confusing 30 wheels back. But I wasn't thinking about winning. I was thinking about surviving and about a respectful end to my two years of wearing this fabulously storied rainbow jersey.

The noise around the circuit didn't let up for a second, and even as the intensity of the race increased, it was impossible to miss the huge number of Slovak fans who had made the trip to Norway. Flags of my home country arched impossibly high into the sky on huge poles. Every time I heard my name shouted, I felt a little stronger. Every Slovak scream from the roadside reminded me that there was an entire nation at home urging me forward, praying for the impossible to happen. There were thousands of Viking helmets covered in red, white, and blue Norwegian colors, huge mountains of men waving flares, hot dogs, or cans of beer. The smell of sizzling frankfurters or the charring of smoked fish was never absent, just shifting in curtains of scent as you passed from one group to another. Swiss fans rang implausibly large cowbells. No cow would survive a night on the Matterhorn with one of those things round her neck. Union Jacks were in abundance too, a budget airline flight for a fantastic weekend was too much for the fanatical British supporters to pass up. Groups of French and Italian supporters crystallized into passionate smaller gangs extolling the praises of one or another particular rider, matching T-shirts imploring Tony Gallopin or Warren Barguil or Gianni Moscon or Sonny Colbrelli to deliver them a rainbow jersey.

I'd got used to wearing that jersey myself over the past 24 months and realized that I was now without the life and energy that it brings to a rider. I was another cyclist in unfamiliar national colors in the middle of a big pack as it surged past, neither Peter Sagan nor the UCI World Champion, just another feather in the eagle's flapping wings. I didn't hear the "Peter!" or "Sagan!" shouts that the rainbow stripes bring, especially being this far from the head of the race. It suited me to be anonymous, but if I thought that perception of anonymity stretched from the crowd to my rivals, then I was kidding myself. They knew I was still there and not warming my toes in the pits or in a nice hot bath at the hotel.

Two climbs of Salmon Hill remained. As we hit it for the penultimate time, the Netherlands injected an acceleration in the race as Tom Dumoulin smashed it up the road in true long-levered Dutch time-trialist style. The bunch was suddenly in a long line and halved in size. That was the last bus stop on the route for many, and they coasted in, their races run. But I was still there against all my expectations. With a lap to go. That guy started clanging that bell to tell us what we already knew. I'm wearing No. 1, but my last half hour as world champion was at hand.

Before the race, a lot of people had been talking about Julian Alaphilippe. This young French guy had already made a big mark on the sport with some daring attacks—precociously confident race-changing efforts—and had quickly obtained the respect of his more-garlanded and experienced Quick-Step teammates. His breakthrough season was 2015, when he was second to me at the Tour of California and also second at both La Flèche Wallonne and (most eyebrow-raising) Liège–Bastogne–Liège. For somebody to come so close to winning a Monument as long and as difficult as the world's oldest bike race at the age of 22 is incredible. His career looked a bit like mine at first glance, but a proper look would show that he was a more accomplished climber than me with a lightning-quick uphill jump in his locker.

It was Alaphilippe who showed us a clean pair of carbon-fiber-soled shoes on the slopes of Salmon Hill the last time. The French were going mad. I was about 20 wheels back, trying to figure out what was going on. I could see a couple of favorites, maybe Philippe Gilbert or Niki Terpstra, trying to bridge, but I wasn't sure. I didn't know if we'd caught all the breakaways either. Confusion reigned, and there were just 10 kilometers left.

I can't tell you how difficult it is to react to changes of pace after 250 kilometers compared to 150 kilometers, which is closer to the distance of, say, your average Grand Tour sprinters' stage. It's like a different sport. I looked around, still flabbergasted that I wasn't one of those hopping off the bus, and saw plenty of fast guys left in with me. Matteo Trentin,

Fernando Gaviria, Michael Matthews, Alexander Kristoff, Edvald Boasson Hagen, Ben Swift . . . these were all genuine bunch gallopers. That wasn't good. At this stage of a long, hard race, I'd be really desperate for a breakaway group to be caught as I'd expect to be one of the fastest left. But I couldn't guarantee an edge over these guys at my best, let alone when I'd been crouched over the hotel toilet a few hours earlier. Sure, I felt surprisingly OK now, but I had zero idea what would happen when I tried to sprint.

I tested my legs by showing my face at the front of the bunch for the first time since the start line six hours ago. The conventional wisdom with cornering on a bike is that you brake first, cut across the apex, then accelerate out. Trial and error—quite a few errors—have taught me that if you take it wide, you don't need to brake, you get a sort of slingshot effect and come out quicker than the others. With Ben Swift trying to close the gap to however many riders were up the road, I used the technique to get up to him and try to affect the chase. Instantly, I remembered what it was like to be Peter Sagan as the race rode up to my wheel . . . and stayed there. Didn't they want to catch these guys? There were about 4 kilometers to go now. Five minutes left as world champion.

I reckon there must have been about 15 guys left in my group. Later, we discovered that the TV coverage dropped out at this point, causing confusion and desperation at the finish and leading to fingernail destruction on an epic scale among the crowds and support staff.

With no visual evidence, I could probably spin you a yarn at this point about how I moved up alongside the bunch pulling a one-handed wheelie and launched a devastating attack that left everybody miles behind. I stopped on the penultimate corner to drink a beer and let them all catch up as I felt so bad at ruining everybody's day.

The truth was that there was almost as much confusion in the bunch as there was in front of the blank television screen. As the finish sucked us nearer, we passed Vasil Kiryienka and my BORA-hansgrohe teammate Lukas Pöstlberger, representing Austria. Was that it? No. I hadn't seen Alaphilippe. And I'm sure that I'd seen at least one Colombian farther up the road, either Rigoberto Urán or Fernando Gaviria or even both of them. Oh! Who's that Danish guy? Who is actually leading this race? And will we catch them?

Just bury it, Peter, I told myself. You sprint for the line and worry about the position after. We were rocketing along the harbor now, and there was a left-hander then a right-hander, then a straight shot of about 300 meters to the finish line. My heart was in my mouth, I could taste blood. You're this close, Peter. Don't die wondering.

Alberto Bettiol was flat out on the front, and it was clear that this was the beginning of the sprint. Nothing cagey here. Everybody was on their own personal limit after six and a half hours, it still wasn't clear if anybody was left out in front, and the earpiece that linked me to Ján Valach in the Slovakia team car behind us wasn't helping as the dropout in live coverage had left the support caravan just as confused as those of us racing. There was no possibility of slowing down to look at my rivals. Bettiol was doing an amazing job for his fastest remaining Italian teammate, Matteo Trentin, but it was working for all of us who wanted to sprint. Shit, I don't think I've ever been traveling so fast on a bike after 267 kilometers. I've hardly ever ridden 267 kilometers in my life, let alone felt like sprinting at the end of it.

I couldn't hear myself think. The noise was insane. Prime reason was the man I'd positioned myself directly behind: Alexander Kristoff. This could be a career-defining moment for the local guy. He was seriously fast, especially when he could wind his powerful sprint up from a distance, and he had a great knack of holding his top speed. I'd looked at him, Trentin, Matthews, and all the others and decided that if I'd been betting on the winner, it would be Kristoff all the way. Really, he had been my favorite ever since the venue was announced years ago—I wasn't going to change my mind with 500 meters to go.

We swung left. The way the yelling went up a notch, the way all those Viking screams spilled onto the circuit as Kristoff began his long acceleration, left me in no doubt that all the breakaways and attacks had come to nothing. We were sprinting for the right to wear that UCI rainbow jersey for a whole year to come. My UCI rainbow jersey. I like you, Alexander, you're one of the good guys, but that is my jersey.

He judged the last 90-degree right-hander perfectly, already sprinting flat out. Bettiol was spent. My slingshot cornering technique was negated by Kristoff's speed, but behind me I could sense a gap opening to Matthews, Trentin, and the others. They'd expected the sprint to open after the corner, and Kristoff's clever acceleration had caught everybody out. It was me and him now. I just had to get past this big Norwegian guy. I'd done it before. But he'd done me before, too.

Three hundred meters is a hell of a long way to ride flat out. If it had been Mark Cavendish leading, I would have been confident of winning if only I could hold his wheel through his initial explosive acceleration. If there had been 20 of us fighting for space, I might have fancied my ability to find a hole to push my nose through. But this was a big wide road with just the two of us going mano a mano for gold, and this guy was the fastest there was on a long, straight road.

I didn't think it was possible for it to be any louder, but the volume went up again. It seemed the whole nation was screaming in Kristoff's ears, blowing him over the line. After pushing myself to breaking point to hold his wheel in that opening 100 meters, I tried to use his slipstream to fire past. Oh Jesus, he was just too fast. My absolute final tank-emptying effort brought me up alongside him, but that barrel-of-a-gun bang that fires you around the last guy in a sprint just wasn't happening. I was alongside him, but the slipstream effect was spent, and he still had his nose in front. With two meters to go, he must be world champion.

At the Tour de France in 2016 in Bern, Switzerland, I had beaten Kristoff by the width of a tire, purely because I'd managed to "throw" my bike at the line at the right moment while he was still concentrating on sprinting. Remembering Switzerland, with all my might I thrust my arms forward, my backside hung out behind the saddle. My legs were straight, my arms were straight, Kristoff was a mirror image on my left.

I waited beyond the finish line, gulping in lungfulls of air and searching for any sign of a result. Had I given enough? Had I left it too late? Every second felt impossibly drawn out as I frantically looked around for any indication of a decision. Finally the finish-line photo came through, and it was clear: His front wheel was a sliver of racing rubber short of mine as we hit the line.

A huge swelling of Slovak fans burst the security line and rushed toward me, screaming, hugging, cheering. They were so thrilled for me and I was for them. We'd achieved the impossible . . . me, Juraj, my national teammates, these incredible fans, everyone back home. World champion three times in a row. One set of a UCI rainbow jersey and gold medal in the Americas, one in the Middle East, one in Scandinavia. Nobody had ever done those things before. And here was a supposedly crazy, supposedly feral kid from an ice-hockey-playing country that had only been independent of its bigger neighbors for 25 years. How the hell did that happen?

PART ONE

Richmond

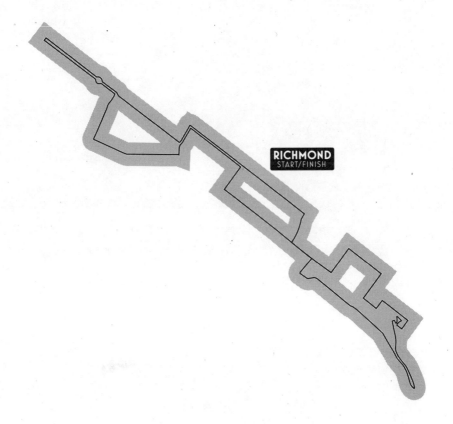

RICHMOND
START/FINISH

WINTER

If there are a hundred riders on the start line of a race, there will be a hundred stories to be told at the end. A hundred careers could yield a hundred different books. Everybody is remarkable, but nobody is special.

I tell you this at the beginning of my story because it's important to remember that everybody has a story. Mine isn't more important than anybody else's, but it is different. Just like everybody else's story is different from mine, and different from each other's.

My story has changed since the start of my career. It's changed over the past three years, and it will change over the next. It will change before I get to the end of this book, as will yours. Let's face it, some of our stories will have changed while I've been writing this sentence.

What I'm trying to say is that I can't tell you my life story because my life is happening and changing every day, just like yours, just like everybody's. I'm only 28, so I'm hoping to be sitting in a big leather armchair, smoking a smelly pipe, and stroking what's left of my wispy white hair by the time I tell my life story. One thing I can certainly tell you is what it has been like to be UCI World Road Race Champion for three years, and that's something that you can only hear from me, I suppose. Nobody else has been champion for three years in a row.

———

Life can change in the blink of an eye. Doors close, doors open. You can win, or you can crash. You can fall in love, or you can lose somebody close to you in an instant.

Even with that undeniable truth in mind, January of 2015 saw me standing at a significant crossroads.

I was 24 years old. I was from Žilina, Slovakia, but now I lived in Monte Carlo. I'd been a professional cyclist for five years, in which time I'd won 65 bike races, been champion of my country four times, and won three green jerseys in the Tour de France.

But now, for the first time in my career, I was changing teams.

I suppose I ought to go back a bit further to explain how I got to this moment. Back to the beginning.

———

As a kid, I loved riding my bike and winning races. People love the stories about me turning up to races on bikes borrowed from my sister or bought for a few koruna from a supermarket, wearing trainers and a T-shirt, and beating everybody. I'm not saying those stories aren't true, but really, they weren't such a big deal. Slovakia was an emerging country, booming after decades dozing behind the Iron Curtain, and now let loose from our awkward embrace with the Czechs thanks to the universally popular "Velvet Divorce." All of us kids were living the high life and screaming at the top of our lungs. I had two older brothers, Milan and Juraj, and there was my sister, Daniela. My dad would drive me all over the place to race bikes. Way beyond Žilina and beyond Slovakia, too: Poland, the Czech Republic, Austria, Slovenia, Italy . . . we'd just go. Mountain bikes, road bikes, cyclocross bikes—it didn't matter. I just wanted to race. Because I was winning, and I liked it.

I was winning enough races that the professional teams started to take notice. In my last year as a junior, I went for testing with Quick-Step at their academy, which had nurtured so much young talent over the years. I stayed at the anonymous building that could easily be mistaken for a factory or the regional office of a nondescript company, knowing that the corridors of this place had echoed with the young voices of many champions over the past 20 years or so. In the end, it was those huge numbers of young cyclists that became an obstacle in my progress. They process literally hundreds of kids through there every year and keep tabs on thousands more juniors across the globe, hoping to unearth the next Merckx, Kelly, or Indurain. Neither my race results nor the numbers I produced in their tests were enough to lift me clear of the other hopeful juniors. They told me to work hard in the Under-23 category for the next couple of seasons, and they would continue to monitor my progress.

It wasn't meant to be negative, but it felt like it. Which is why, when the Liquigas team came along and said they'd take me on board straightaway, I couldn't wait to say yes. They didn't need to wait for me, and I sure as hell wasn't going to wait for a call from Quick-Step that might never come.

There were quotas on Under-23 teams in Italy regarding foreign riders, so I carried on riding in the Slovakian national setup for mountain bike and road races from Slovakia to Italy to Germany to Croatia. I might not have been riding the Tour de France in a Liquigas jersey, but I was 19, and I was a pro-continental cyclist earning 1,000 euros a month. It was pretty cool.

In July 2009, Liquigas called me up to meet the main squad at the Tour of Poland. Led by Ivan Basso, there were some guys there whom I would become close to over the years, guys like Maciej Bodnar; Daniel Oss, who is back with me at BORA-hansgrohe now; but most of all Sylwester Szmyd, who has been a good friend for many years and is now my coach.

The introduction was Liquigas's way of telling me: "You're in." Even though I was still only 19, there were to be no more Under-23 races, no more barreling round Europe in a Slovakia jersey, no more mountain bike racing. I was to be a full-time professional on the ProTour circuit.

———

Liquigas got me an apartment in San Donà di Piave near Venice. It was small, but it was mine. My brother Juraj came to stay, and so did Maroš Hlad, my soigneur from back home. This was the beginning of Team Peter, a little unit of friends who could all rely on each other in any situation. I now had an agent, too: Giovanni Lombardi, a classy ex-rider who'd led out Erik Zabel to many of his green jersey victories. Giovanni, or Lomba as we affectionately call him, was the first to see the potential of Team Peter and the one man who has done more than anybody else to make it a reality. The first real appointment of Team Peter was to bring Juraj on board as a pro at Liquigas, and that was thanks to Giovanni. He knew my brother was good enough to hold a pro contract in his own right, but he also knew he would fight like crazy to protect me on the bike and off it, too. Juraj, Maroš, and I stayed together in Veneto, moving closer to the mountains so we could vary our training more. They were great days, and we were there for two years until I moved to Monaco on Giovanni's advice.

My first race as a professional was the Tour Down Under in 2010. I'd never been to Adelaide before, but I wasn't completely unfamiliar with Australia. Four months earlier I had raced at the 2009 UCI Mountain Bike World Championships in the nation's capital, Canberra, where I took fourth in the U23 men category. I loved the heat of Adelaide in January, riding out every day in shorts and a jersey without having to worry about arm warmers or the like. It's another country with its own distinctive smell. Eucalyptus, or gum trees, as the locals say. If I catch a scent of that anywhere in the world, I'm transported back to sunny days in the southern hemisphere, those hot days where the earth seems to be flattened by the heat from above.

It's a gentle race to do, too. As well as the weather, there are no long transfers between stages, no packing your bag every day, and a nice hotel that the whole race is staying at. As with any career, there are tedious parts to life as a pro cyclist. Somehow, during the Tour Down Under, those elements are less apparent. As I've grown older, I've appreciated the laid-back nature of Australians in general, too. Nothing is too much of a problem. They have a look in their eyes that seems to say: Why so serious?

There was a bit of rough and tumble down under. I raced, sprinted, fell off, but overall thought, *Well, if I'm only 20 and have never raced before, and these guys are all 30-something and have been doing it for years, I reckon I might be able to win a few of these one day.*

I thought that day had come as soon as we got back to Europe. I wasn't meant to be riding a big race like Paris–Nice this soon, but Bodnar was sick, and the team decided to throw me in for the experience with no expectation of me. Central France was freezing, but on just the second stage into Limoges, there was a crash 500 meters from the line as the different sprint trains got in each other's way. As ever, I was sprinting on my own, watching the wheels, and the crash left me with a gap. I smashed straight through it, heading for the line, but just as I thought I was going to be a winner for the first time, I realized that I'd gone too soon, and the quick Frenchman William Bonnet came over me with the line in sight.

I was disappointed for about two minutes, but then I realized that I had nearly won in my first European race, and a big race at that. The wins would surely come.

And they did. The first one was the following day when I won from a small group after our attacks had whittled down the peloton over some hilly country. It was like being back in Žilina: a flat grey sky that seemed to merge with the horizon and snow flurries that caused the stage start to be brought forward 50 kilometers into the race.

Three days later I was at it again; this time attacking 3 kilo-meters out when everybody was waiting for the sprint and arriving in Aix-en-Provence two seconds before everybody else. The question that I would hear from the press most days in my pro career was asked for the first time that afternoon: Was I a sprinter or not?

That Paris–Nice gave me my first points jersey, too. As I stood on the podium next to Alberto Contador, who had won the race with his usual attacking panache, I thought: *You could get used to this, Peter.*

———

I picked up another points jersey at the Tour of California, and the season flew by. A year later and I was picking up that Cali-fornian green jersey again, then taking three stages in my first Grand Tour, the Vuelta, where I managed to complete the whole three weeks. In all, I won 15 races in 2011 and 16 more in 2012.

The spring of 2012 was when I was really able to make my presence felt at the classics, where I was unable to get a win but finished in the top ten at Milan–San Remo, Gent–Wevelgem, and the Tour of Flanders, and even managed to get on the podium at a hilly race like Amstel Gold. I was being asked if becoming a classics specialist was blunting my sprint, but that was just daft. Sprinting to win a stage of a race where most of the combatants' first priority is to get through to the next day unscathed is an entirely different proposition to taking a Monument like Flanders or Roubaix home with you. For a start, it's a case of "shit or bust." You win, or you go home; there's no second chance waiting tomorrow, meaning that crazy do-or-die efforts are the order of the day. Add to that the distance of each race. Milan–San Remo can be 300 kilometers long, and the bunch smashes it out of Milan and over the Turchino Pass like greyhounds out of the traps. The stamina that's needed to be strong after seven hours of racing is not the same as the stamina a track cyclist needs to blast past somebody on the Olympic Velodrome after a couple of laps. Suddenly "sprinter" is a much more complicated term than it would originally appear.

The last tool in the locker that you need for classics success is experience. The classics are steeped in history, with every berg, corner, or stretch of cobbles known like the streets around their homes by the men, like Cancellara or Boonen, who have been winning them for many years. In contrast, most stage races are a moveable feast. When you come to a finish in the Tour de France, you'll be trying to remember the roadbook from when you looked at it in the team bus for the first and last time that morning. Is there a bend? Was that corner a left- or a right-hander? How far from there to the line? Is it uphill? Will there be a headwind?

Put all that together and you just need one thing: all the luck in the world.

I got an opportunity to show the world that I could sprint in July when I went to the Tour de France for the first time.

On a night out in Žilina with Milan and all my old friends, for some reason—and that reason is probably beer—we were all doing a chicken dance: elbows out, knees out, waddling round the bar like the overgrown teenagers we were. Now, as Gabriele Uboldi, my road manager, will be the first to tell you, seeing as he is so often on the wrong end of them, I am always motivated by a wager. When the first stage of the Tour hit the Côte de Seraing, one of the steep ramps that Liège–Bastogne–Liège goes over each year, all I could think of was that if I hit the top first, I could do the chicken dance over the finish line like I'd promised the guys at home.

Fabian Cancellara went for broke on the lower slopes, and I nearly popped my eyeballs out to get on his wheel. He was wearing the yellow jersey by virtue of winning the prologue the previous day and was determined to make it two wins out of two. As I got up to him on the steepest bit of the climb, I looked back and saw that only Edvald Boasson Hagen had made it with us. The rest of the Tour was stuck to the lower slopes. As we reached the top, with a few hundred meters left, Cancellara tried hard to get me to do a turn, but I kept my head down on his wheel, knowing that if I could get him to lead out, I fancied my chances of coming around him. Boasson Hagen was similarly glued to my wheel, probably thinking the same thing, and the bunch was closing in. Just when I thought I might lose my nerve and attack, fearing we would be caught with 200 meters to go, thankfully Cancellara opened up the sprint.

He did so at the perfect moment for me, just before the pace dropped off, and I soared around him to take my first Tour de France stage win, freewheeling enough to be able to do the chicken dance all the way over the line. Cancellara wasn't happy with me, initially because he felt I had ridden his coattails to the win, which was true, but he was a superstar, and I was a rookie. Then that celebration really got up his nose, taking it as a personal snub and a sign of disrespect.

By the time we reached Paris, I had my first Tour de France green jersey, and I'd been able to add the Incredible Hulk and the Running Man to my celebrations. I would have won more, but I'd run out of ideas for victory salutes. At least Cancellara knew by then it was nothing personal.

The 2013 season was my best year to date, picking up 22 wins in all sorts of races on all sorts of terrain, making me the most successful cyclist on the ProTour circuit that year. Or should I say the "winningest," like the Americans? It's a horrible word, but it's more accurate. Who is to say that winning 22 races is more successful than winning one Tour de France and 17 other races, like Chris Froome did that year?

I'd initially thought it was going to be the year of the second place when I went through March with second at Strade Bianche, Milan–San Remo, E3 Harelbeke, and the Tour of Flanders. Planted in the middle of that run was my first classics win. At last. Belgium was bitterly cold and apparently Gent–Wevelgem was nearly cancelled, but instead it was shortened by 50 kilometers. That obviously suited me, what with stamina (in my opinion) being the older riders' strength, and I found myself at the sharp end of the race all day. With 4 kilometers to go and my breakaway rivals wondering how they were going to beat me in the sprint, I attacked instead and won on my own, popping some wheelies to please the crowd who'd been risking hypothermia to see me win.

———

I suppose in retrospect, 2014 wasn't so bad, with a third Tour de France points jersey in a row to show for my troubles and seven wins along the way, but in truth it was hellish. I was realistic enough to know that my upward trajectory to this point had been such that I might need to take stock. I was well-known now and heavily marked whenever I raced, which was bound to bring my win numbers down a bit. I was focusing more and more on the big titles like Flanders and Roubaix, which are always going to be harder to win—that's the whole point—and everyone needs a bit of luck. I could even deal with treading water for a season if that's what it was going to take to move on in the longer term.

But this wasn't treading water. This was shit. I was rubbish. I was exhausted all the time. I had won that Tour green jersey again, but 2014 was the first time I'd ridden a Tour de France and not won a stage. No silly celebrations. Shit, no normal celebrations. I felt I was letting everybody down: my friends, my family, Team Peter, my teammates, Cannondale (as Liquigas had become), everybody.

It was time for a change. Either that or go home to Žilina and give up.

On Slovakia

I love Slovakia. There's something exciting about coming from such a young and proud country, like you're always doing things for the first time. It's a crazy way to think, really. Slovak people have been here for the thick end of two thousand years, and we've got our own language and our own distinct style of medieval architecture that you'd recognize immediately.

But living memory is a bit different. We spent most of the twentieth century being pulled between the competing might of Germany and the Soviet Union, and more often than not, we were paired up with our Czech neighbors. We were finally parted from them without the need for much more than a handshake and a wave in 1993, a process so without acrimony that it's popularly known as the Velvet Divorce. We still share a lot of stuff with the Czechs. After all, they make the beer, so there's absolutely nothing to be gained in falling out with them. Oh, and we're in the European Union, too. I'm looking forward to one of my British friends effectively explaining to me why leaving it is such a good idea. I've been waiting a little while now.

There are about 5 million of us Slovaks, which puts us in the same ballpark as Norway, Finland, and Ireland by population—yes, I can use Google and Wikipedia, thank you—but we're short on national heroes whether in history, art, or sport, so it's a very cool thing for us to have a world champion in anything. I do feel a certain mixture of pressure and pride. You can't avoid it, not when everybody in the street wants to shake your hand or take a selfie with you, and I'm not going to be the miser who denies them. I'd want one. And as there's only 5 million of us, I'm working my way through everyone who wants one quite systematically. It's not so much that I'm super famous or anything like that, but more to do with us not having too many famous people, if you see what I mean. We don't, as a rule, go in for celebrity culture much in Slovakia. It's not like you get people throwing themselves at your feet or silly stuff like that; we're all just people getting on with our lives.

———

Would I be the rider I am today if I hadn't grown up in Slovakia? That's a really interesting question. I'm always being asked about my antics on a bike. I mean, the way I ride my bike and do tricks, wheelies, stunts, avoid crashes, that sort of thing. In fact, I'm usually being told, "Peto, no wonder you can do wheelies; it's because you used to do BMX. Hey Peter, you can park your bike in a roof rack on top of a car because you were a mountain biker."

These things are true to a certain extent. You need a whole new set of skills to ride mountain bikes and BMX. But I had a lot of those skills before I even started doing those things. In my opinion, the most useful education for being a professional athlete, pretty much any sport, is a childhood spent outdoors, and as a youngster I was given free rein to explore and play in the Slovakian countryside. Other families probably thought I was wild . . . climbing trees, hiking out through the forests, swimming in the lakes and rivers, and building dens and camps in summer. Then in winter we would be skiing, sledding, and organizing the world's largest snowball fights.

While you think you're just having fun and being a tearaway, you're learning crafts and skills. Coordination is probably the most obvious one, but you're building your strength, finding out what your body can do, discovering your limits, and then trying to reset them to a higher level. You're training, really, whether you want to be a soccer player, an ice hockey player, or a cyclist. Often, when I'm hurtling down a mountainside or testing my nerves in a fiercely contested bunch sprint, I'm drawing on childhood experiences with my big brothers in the Slovakian countryside.

———

I'm not Slovakia's first cycling champion. That accolade belongs to Ján Valach. He was a Slovak guy riding on international teams and competing in big races up until 2010, and he was the only guy we had to look up to when we were coming through the ranks. But more than that, Ján always had the ability to see the bigger picture, which made him the perfect man to drag Slovakian cycling up by its bootstraps and really make something of the national setup. He has been behind the wheel of the car at each of my world championship victories, and now I'm lucky enough to have him with us in the BORA-hansgrohe team, too.

Unfortunately, those perceptive directeur sportif (DS) roles at Richmond, Doha, and Bergen are only part of the story, and the other half is sadly the narrative of my Slovakia as I see it today.

Ján started getting involved in cycling administration well before he stopped riding. He could see that there was little vision involved in Slovakian cycling, and what organization there was resembled a village party. Internationally, we were a joke, with Juraj and I and the others like us relying on the dedication of our parents to pull things together and to drive us to races all over central Europe. My contemporary Michal Kwiato remembers getting to junior races in, say, Croatia with the Polish squad and their matching bikes and kits, and so forth, then I'd be getting out of the back seat of my dad's car with my bike wheels tucked under my feet and my cycling shoes wedged under the passenger seat.

Ján was determined to put a stop to that and demanded that the money received by the federation went into the grassroots of the sport. You can imagine that the suits holding the purse strings weren't so keen on diverting funds away from their own little clubs and races. There were other scandals too—the national velodrome was sold off to a developer on the understanding that the cash would go into a new state-of-the-art facility. Needless to say, we're still waiting. In the end, a man can only bang his head against a brick wall so many times, and Ján withdrew from the sharp end and put all his energy into being the DS for the national squad, but that is the role where he has been able to have the most impact on my career, even if his vision for Slovakian cycling continues to gather dust.

The thing I am most proud of here is the Peter Sagan Academy. I set it up after talking with Ján and hearing about how the national cycling program ought to be improved and how he met resistance at every turn.

Three years ago, I took on the junior cycling team that I'd grown up with to say thank you and to try to give a chance to other kids coming through. We rebranded it the Peter Sagan Academy to give it a bit of weight, and I invested some money in it. With my name on the academy, it was easier for them to bring in some other sponsors, too. The national federation was still expecting parents to pay for their kids to race or drive their kids across Europe themselves. These days, thanks to crucial sponsorship from Robert Spinazzè, CEO of the Spinazzè Group (they make the concrete poles and structures used to protect orchards and vineyards), we're able to run a program to take boys and girls between the ages of 8 and 18 to the same races that the German, Italian, and Polish national structures are targeting. Robert is passionate about the sport, and his involvement is essential as we continue our quest for future champions. Sportful, the clothing manufacturer, has joined us to supply all the clothing for the academy and the team, and without their support, our ambitions would be impeded. We've added an Under-23 layer now, too, so that we can continue their development further and keep the teams together. The ultimate aim is to have many more Slovakian riders in the professional peloton and maybe one day a ProTour team based in Slovakia. We are now supporting 85 riders at the academy, and I believe it will stand on its own soon when the top teams start benefiting from the talent it is beginning to supply. There is no pressing need for the big cycling teams to invest in youth in the same way that football clubs across Europe do. Those are short-lived commercial enterprises with short-term goals. A grassroots program like this could make a real difference. Any number of factors can take promising kids away from the game: the need to earn money or study for better-paying careers, or other sports with better investment creaming off the talent.

Then there's the Peter Sagan Kids Tour, which has been running in earnest since 2014. Now these are awesome events, and every time I'm able to attend, I have an absolute blast. The Tour is run by my first-ever coach, Peter Zánický. When I was just 9 years old, Peter used to drive Juraj and me to events all over the country, and it is so reassuring to know that my old coach now has nearly five thousand enthusiastic children turning up to compete and have a fun day out. These days the Kids Tour consists of nine events from March to September, each taking place in a beautiful Slovak town. It's so heartwarming to see kids as young as toddlers scooting along on their balance bikes at an organized occasion like this. There's a competitive element to every event, but the main focus is on creating a family-friendly day out with the emphasis on having fun! So far, thousands of kids have taken part, and, while I'm positive there are a number of future stars among them, it's the smiles on their faces that make the whole enterprise particularly gratifying.

I'd like to think that any Slovak youngster looking to take up cycling as a career would have an easier time of it than we did. And who knows, perhaps one day I'll be the guy in the car urging on the next Slovak world champion. History has this funny way of repeating itself.

SPRING

Oleg Tinkov is a funny bastard in so many ways. Funny in that he's always playing the fool, or telling stories, or goofing around. Funny because he just can't stop himself from saying the things that really shouldn't be said. But also funny in that he's just not wired up like other people.

It wasn't Oleg Tinkov who brought me to the Tinkoff team, like you might think. The prime mover behind my decision to change teams for the first time in my career was Bjarne Riis.

Riis had been running a cycling team pretty much since the day he'd retired. He won the Tour de France in 1996, then rode alongside Jan Ullrich as his younger teammate took the victory the following year. Soon afterward he was instrumental in setting up the Danish team that would go on to become CSC and then Saxo Bank, winning most things that could be won at some point during the team's existence. He had a reputation for getting the best out of riders who might have otherwise ridden out less stellar careers or even disappeared altogether. He sounded like a great fit for me. After bringing Tinkov in originally as a sponsor, he'd recently sold the team organization itself to the Russian oligarch, but he was continuing to work for the team as the head honcho on a three-year contract.

Giovanni had been fielding calls from BMC, Sky, Quick-Step, and the racing driver Fernando Alonso, who was apparently putting together a top-level team, all of whom were interested in taking Team Peter on board for 2015. In the end, though, through all the talk and noise, only Tinkoff was prepared to negotiate to a positive result. With the good feeling I was getting from Riis and the decisive actions of his team, it was the only choice to make. Giovanni had seen out his riding career under Riis and had been a teammate of his a few years before that, and he hadn't a bad word to say about the Dane. Serious, trustworthy, engaged, and knowledgeable. New team, new people, new system, new bikes . . . new motivation.

Giovanni worked hard to ensure that the whole of Team Peter would be absorbed into the Tinkoff organization. That was easier said than done. There were riders and soigneurs who had been there for years who would have to be placated if all the various arms of Team Peter were to be accommodated. In the end, Juraj and Maroš came with me.

Suddenly we were part of a bigger setup, with a more professional approach, and with the bigger expectations and pressures that involves.

The UCI had been implementing stricter rules on coaches in an effort to make sure that riders' health was being correctly protected and any possible fluctuations in performance due to doping would be more likely to be flushed out. To be honest, one of the things that had been grinding me down at Cannondale was having to report to a guy every day with all my numbers: training figures, heart rates, power output, calories taken, number of breaths, how many pisses . . . It was doing my head in, but I knew it had to be done, and I put myself at the mercy of my new team. Bjarne Riis hooked me up with Bobby Julich, a rider who had hit great heights with him at CSC and was now a well-respected coach.

I talked with Bobby every day. "How do you feel, Peter? What did you do today, Peter? What was your resting rate, Peter? What was your training rate, Peter? How did you sleep, Peter? What did you eat, Peter? What color was your shit, Peter?"

Right in the middle of trying to come to terms with this new and intrusive way of working, the shit really hit the fan at Tinkoff. It was clear that there was a bit of a power struggle going on between Bjarne and Oleg for control of the team. I didn't really know either of them or anybody at the team, so I didn't know whether it was normal or not, though some of the older hands were convinced it had grown worse since Bjarne had sold the whole operation to Oleg. Later, Bjarne would claim that Oleg was jealous of his close relationship with the riders and staff, while Oleg thought that Bjarne saw him as nothing more than a cash provider, funding everything Bjarne wanted and getting treated like a mug in return. As usual in things like this, the truth was somewhere in the middle. They were certainly completely different characters: Bjarne considered every word before delivering it and thought laughing an unnecessary expense of energy. Oleg had no filter between brain and mouth, and every thought he had ended up in the wide world, no matter how offensive or outrageous. People probably think I'm more like Oleg, but in truth I am very uncomfortable with rudeness, either in myself or other people. My dad never let me get away with it when I was a kid, and it stuck. Beyond my public persona as a "crazy character," I always try to be polite.

We were at Tirreno–Adriatico in March 2015. Oleg wanted us to be pushing every day. We had Alberto Contador as leader, and Oleg wanted us to be challenging Nairo Quintana for leadership of the race at every moment, while Bjarne was all for taking a more cautious approach so early in the season. He gestured to the points jersey that I was wearing and the couple of stages I had won, but basically ignored Oleg. And there is nothing Oleg hates more than being ignored. After one stage, Oleg came to the team hotel in the evening to exert his authority. He was furious to discover that Bjarne had gone out for dinner with friends elsewhere. After kicking lumps out of furniture for a couple of hours, he finally confronted Bjarne, completely oblivious, when he showed up outside the team bus. They had a raging argument right then and there in front of everyone. There were other teams, race officials, and journalists present, you name it.

After the race, I was feeling OK. A bit fatigued, but I figured all this hard work so early in the season was good preparation for the classics. As ever, the first of these would be Milan–San Remo—La Classicissma, La Primavera, and a race I thought I could win—in just a few days, so instead of going back to Monte Carlo, my girlfriend, Katarina, and I went to stay with Bjarne and his family at his place in Switzerland. I was still tired all the time, but it was a great handful of days: riding on hard, clean surfaces, not much traffic, calm guidance from Bjarne, and lovely food at his house in the evening. Plus, because I was with Bjarne, I didn't have to speak to Bobby every two minutes: "What does your piss smell like today, Peter? Can you count the hairs on your big toe for me, Peter?"

On the Friday morning after a beautiful dinner the night before, we said our good-byes and arranged to meet in Milan the following day.

Saturday arrived, but Bjarne didn't. Confusion and rumors began to spread through the team. Where was Bjarne? What had happened? Had Oleg had enough? At dinner in the team hotel that night, the news broke officially: Bjarne had been fired and removed from his post with immediate effect.

At the team meeting, the riders were like a cross between a bunch of old women wailing and wringing their hands at a funeral and kids in the school playground after somebody has kicked the ball over the fence into the garden. "What are we going to do? What are we going to doooooo?"

"Guys, come on," I said. "It's just a bike race, you know? *Che cazzo?* It's not like Bjarne was going to ride our bikes for us. We get up in the morning. We put warm clothes on. We ride up over the Turchino Pass. We get down to the Riviera. We take our jackets and legwarmers off. We ride over the capi. We sprint into San Remo. It's pretty simple."

It was indeed pretty simple, and as we came to the finale, I was in with a big shout. Alexander Kristoff had Luca Paolini lead him out for a long sprint, as he prefers. He's really fast when he gets rolling, but he lacks that explosive Cavendish-style punch. I tried to respond, but 290 kilometers is a hell of a long way in

March, especially when you've been training yourself half to death, and my legs let me know loud and clear that they strongly disapproved of sprinting. Only John Degenkolb could get past Kristoff, and Michael Matthews edged me off the podium. Oh well, at least it was a short drive home.

———

Great. So now the guy who had brought me here had disappeared. But not after burdening me with a coach who was destroying me week by week. Bobby didn't understand me, and I couldn't stand his persistent interventions.

I'm lucky. I've never had any problem motivating myself to train. If I want to win, I have to race well. And if I want to race well, I have to train. But that is what training is to me: preparation to race. Not training for its own sake. Maybe that works for some riders: G.C. riders, for instance, like Alberto Contador or Chris Froome, who don't race so often, need to train with structure to make sure they arrive at their goals in peak condition. Also, they can use races like the one-week stage races in Spain or the Dauphiné or Tour de Romandie to train. If you take this year, 2018, as a comparison, I won my first race in Australia in January. I'm basically trying to win twice a week pretty much from then until the world's in September with a couple of weeks off here and there for good behavior. Or, in the case of last year, bad behavior, but we'll come to that.

Training to say you're in good shape. Amazing numbers. Wow. Well, as far as I'm aware, no bike race has ever been won on a power meter. Nobody ever got UCI points for wearing the maximum output jersey. Even Chris Froome has to stop looking at his computer and run up mountains in his cycling shoes sometimes. Training for its own sake. That's exactly how it felt with Bobby. He was obsessed with my figures. I had to do exactly as he asked every day and then spend the rest of the day talking to him about it. I was absolutely exhausted and miserable with it. I'd start thinking I'd turn my phone off or pretend I was sick. It was ludicrous. I love training, but this was killing me. Death by numbers.

Every coach I've ever met asks me: "Do you want to be a better climber? A better sprinter? A better time trialer?" I say, why mess with nature? I am what I am. I go OK. If it's not broken, don't fix it. I believe that if you make a drastic change to improve one facet of your performance, there will be a price to pay elsewhere. Riders who have lost weight to climb better lose their kick. People who have improved their stamina become unable to sprint. Becoming more aerodynamic means losing power. The list is endless, and I'm sure you get what I'm talking about.

The basic problem was a pretty simple one. Forget resting heart rate, fat content, power outputs, and training algorithms. I was just plain knackered. Tired beyond belief. But still, I'd drag myself out of the flat in Monaco and cajole myself into riding along, sticking to whatever plan Bobby had set for me that day.

I went to the northern classics and admit I was truly shit. This was meant to be the year when I cracked it: no more second and third steps of the podium, no more near misses. Well, we got that right anyway. I was nowhere near. By the time April blew itself out, I'd forgotten what a podium looked like.

The team was not happy. All sorts of rumors were floating around about what was going wrong. I can't say if Bobby actually said this or not, but I heard he told the team I'd been overraced so much since turning pro, that I was already burnt out. Any results I would ever achieve in my career had already been won. I was finished at 25. A busted flush. A racehorse whose knees had gone.

"That's it," I said. "Fuck it, I quit."

In my mind I was already an ex-professional cyclist on the beach with Katarina. Well, I'd still have some stories to tell about the times I'd had. Maybe I'd write a book one day.

———

Giovanni activated crisis-management mode. To be fair to him, he has only ever tried to support me in what I want to do. There was no pressure to get me out there, no anger or disappointment, only concern that I was OK, and worry that I wouldn't go and do something stupid.

I was a few months into one of the most lucrative contracts the sport had ever seen, and it ran for three years. Turn up, ride, do my best, play my part, and after three years I could retire and support my family comfortably for life. Don't worry about Bobby, don't worry about Oleg, don't worry about the team, don't worry about anything. That was Lomba's job. Surely, wasn't that the point of Team Peter? Relax, man. Why so serious?

In the end, Giovanni's solution was the most sensible one. It was clear I was going to need a new coach, and that man was about to become the next key member of Team Peter. Patxi Vila was already on the staff at Tinkoff, but he was a different type of guy than Bobby. He was a Basque who'd been a pro until pretty recently, without hitting the heights that Bobby had. But perhaps that was a strength for him as a coach. Winners are often so driven that they're not so good at listening to others' needs. A good domestique has to know what his leader wants or he'll never make a good career. Maybe that's a better base for being a coach?

Patxi was very smart at the beginning. "I realized straight-away that you knew what you were doing," he told me. "You ate well, your weight didn't fluctuate much, you had a strong consti-tution that didn't need a lot of attention. Most of all, you'd won a shed-load of races without ever having a coach."

I liked him. He let me get on with it.

"The training plan I worked out with you at the start was just so we had something written down, really," says Patxi now. We're all sitting around remembering these days in the Sierra Nevada where BORA-hansgrohe is doing our customary February training camp before the start of the 2018 classics. It's after dark, it's freezing outside, and the Wi-Fi is terrible, so we might as well sit and talk. "It was clear you had an accurate understanding of your body. I saw my role to support that rather than dismantle it. If you told me that you'd only done one hour instead of four because you felt shitty, I'd know it was the right decision. It was easy."

With Patxi as my coach, I slowly began to relax. In my head, I was already done. I started to think about what was important: health, happiness, being myself, having fun. It's good to have a plan because it points you in the right direction, but you can't expect it to work 100 percent of the time. That's not racing. That's not life. Say you have a plan to be in the first 10 riders with 7 kilometers to go in a race because there's a narrow bit of road and a little hill up ahead. But a hundred other riders have that plan, too. That's 90 people who are going to be disappointed, but what are they going to do? Get off and walk home? You have to adapt. Find another way. Accept what is in front of you and find another way. There are some things that you just can't change, like punctures and crashes. I decided from that point on that I would do my best but accept the results whether good or bad.

If I win, I win. If I crash, I crash. If I come in 30th, I come in 30th. I'll still be Peter at the finish, and the sky won't fall.

That's how it was when I first started out. Then you start winning, start leading, the pressure builds, and one day, somewhere along the way, you lose what it was that helped you win in the first place. Thinking back to my debut at the Tour Down Under, I remembered thinking, I could win one of these. Five years on, I'd lost that feeling. It wasn't just the overtraining, it was the contract negotiations, the uncertainty, the pressure. And then, as if to reassure me that I wasn't completely losing my mind, amid all the tests at Tinkoff, the team doctor said the results showed I'd had a virus slowing me down for much of the previous season. Thank you! It wasn't all me, then. Had Cannondale known? Did they decide not to tell me because they needed me on the start line week in, week out, knowing that I was leaving at the end of the year? I don't know. But they either knew and kept it from me or their medical testing was shit. One of those scenarios had to be true.

I still talked to Patxi most days and filled him in on what I was doing, but the pressure was off completely. All I had to do was get through the 2015 season. I was quitting soon. Why so serious?

By now, I knew how much I liked the Tour of California. I'd been there five times and come back with five green jerseys. The people were always pleased to see you, but they were never in your face. The air smelled clean and held the scent of oranges. The roads were good, the racing was fast but laid-back . . . what wasn't to like?

My road manager, Gabriele, always says that there is something to remind me of Giovanni there, too: The biggest climb was called Mount Baldy. Thanks, Gabriele. Don't worry, I'm sure Lomba will never read this.

Oleg, Bjarne, and Bobby were a world away, as were the disappointments of Roubaix, Flanders, and San Remo.

Mark Cavendish was here, though, and he was on fire, sprinting in that explosive way that only he can and reminding me what a pure sprinter looks like. He showed me a clean pair of heels on the first two stages, and I began to think that my green jersey count would be likely to stick on five. Never mind. It's good to have a plan, but when your plan doesn't work out, you find another way.

Stage 3 was 170 kilometers with six king of the mountain primes and over 3,000 meters of climbing around San Jose. Not a Sagan kind of day at all. So it felt pretty fine to win the kick for second spot; a great long solo effort from a Latvian guy, Toms Skujinš, held us all off for the win.

The next day I was too quick for Cav for once, and I bounced my wheel off the road a couple of times as I crossed the line then pulled a big wheelie to show how pleased I was. Now that I didn't care if I won, I was winning again, and I remembered that I liked it.

After Cav turned the tables again on the next stage, I surprised everyone, including myself, by pulling out a win in the next stage. No surprises in that, you might think, Sagan, you greedy bastard, but hold your horses . . . it was a time trial. In my new mode of not giving a shit, I smashed it round the flat 10-kilometer course to not only take the victory, but also the yellow jersey. Not my usual color, but I liked it.

I liked it so much that on the queen stage to Mount Giovanni, sorry, Mount Baldy, I dug in and finished in the top 10, losing less than a minute to Julian Alaphilippe and coming to the summit ski station in front of climbers like Haimar Zubeldia and Gesink. Alaphilippe had taken the jersey from me by two seconds, but with time bonuses to be won on the final stage, I was still confident.

Ahead of the final stage, we were all gathered round the start line, eagerly anticipating the starter's gun. It was one of the tightest Tours I've ever been involved in, and every rider in contention had been crunching the numbers to calculate how the stage might play out to their advantage. As we were held at the start line, Lomba approached Cav and casually inquired whether he intended to challenge for the intermediate sprints and the bonus seconds that came their way. Since I was just a couple of seconds behind his teammate Alaphilippe, Cav confirmed he would be shelving his own ambitions to help the Frenchman in the G.C. No sooner had he finished answering Lomba's inquiry than his tire exploded! Right in front of him! Surely a good omen for the rest of the day, and an exchange that would have Lomba in hysterics for the rest of the year. To be fair, Cav did storm the sprint to win the stage, and I had no qualms about that—he was flying all week—but nervously I waited to see if I'd pipped Tyler Farrar to third, as that carried a 4-second bonus. As usual, Gabriele was confident and told me not to worry, and sure enough, I'd won the Tour of California.

A retirement present, perhaps.

SUMMER

With sunny miles in my legs and sunny smiles all over my face, I headed to Park City, Utah, for some altitude training as a new man.

Altitude training has proved itself to be a massive benefit for me over the last few years, but 2015 was when it took off. Patxi convinced me of its powers, and he has proved bang on. Plus, I get to hang out in places like Utah, Colorado, and the Sierra Nevada in Spain.

The trick to understanding altitude training and how it can help is to slightly tweak the title. It's not really altitude training; it's living at altitude while training. Hanging out and, most importantly, sleeping where the air is thin means you're using less fuel (oxygen) to carry the load. On the one hand, you're working your body harder to get through whatever you're asking it to do, but you're also teaching it to run more efficiently and make the most of the resources it has available. It's teaching your engine to run leaner. You need to beware of overtraining, though. If you tip over the edge, it takes a long time to climb out of the drop on the other side. Altitude training with Patxi is safest for me because he is so knowledgeable and understands it better than most, but he also trusts me to tell him when I've had enough.

Lots of people say, "sleep high, train low," but I think the second bit is less important. As long as it's training, I don't mind too much if it's up at the top or down at the bottom. In Spain, we sleep high and train low most days as it's bloody freezing up high with icy roads, and it gets pretty busy with skiing traffic on the roads at the weekends. The shape of the Sierra Nevada lends itself to it as well: It's just a huge great lump rising out of the plain. So we hop in the cars in the morning and drive down to Granada to ride. We do a bit of team time trial training with new bikes too, so the quiet roads and warm weather are very handy as there is technical riding to be done, but a fair bit of hanging around too. If it's a nice day, after the session we ride back up to get some climbing in the legs too. It's a 30-kilometer drag, and the road can be pretty busy on Saturdays and Sundays. When you can be on the beach at Motril in 20 degrees Celsius and skiing in reliable powder within a couple of hours, that's not surprising. When it's grim in the mountains, we can usually persuade Patxi that the road along the beach would be the best place to head. As he's a member of the new generation of DSs that like to ride with their teams rather than sit in the car barking out instructions, he's very much up for that kind of training. A coffee. A beer. Why so serious?

There are no beaches in Utah, but I like America, and there is a cool West Coast vibe in Utah that chimes with my Tour of California experiences. I had a great time in Park City. Train hard. Kick back. Repeat.

Back in Europe in June, I went to the Tour of Switzerland, picked up a couple more stages and my fifth points jersey in five appearances there. I then had a brief visit home to Slovakia and got my fifth national road race championship, ensuring I'd have my own personal jersey for another year.

Whether I cared or not, it seemed I was ready for the Tour de France.

———

I would be riding the Tour de France alongside Alberto Contador at Tinkoff. We'd spoken together in the bunch ever since my very first European pro race, Paris–Nice in 2010, and had always got on well. There was no thought in my mind that we might have a problem racing a big event together. There was no need for me to be known as a co-leader or to have another kind of designation that other people might need to make them feel important.

He was the leader. He had proved over many seasons that he was probably the best G.C. rider of his generation. He'd had his problems with the UCI and served a disputed ban, but he still had massive respect in the peloton and a massive point to prove, too. Going into that 2015 race, he had an amazing seven Grand Tour victories, plus two more that the UCI had scratched out for doping. As a result, he was looking for his third legitimate Tour de France win, going up against Sky's Chris Froome, Astana's Vincenzo Nibali, and the Movistar duo of Nairo Quintana and Alejandro Valverde.

In Bjarne Riis's absence, Oleg had promoted Stefano Feltrin to general manager. Previously, Feltrin had been the guy looking after the contracts for the riders, sponsors, and such, and he had a very clear vision of how everything should work.

"You're going to the Tour to work exclusively for Alberto," Feltrin and Steven de Jongh, Tinkoff's head DS, told me.

"No, I can't do that. I have a green jersey to defend and stages to win."

I couldn't understand the logic. I was aware that there had been problems in the past in teams that had conflicting objectives, but I didn't think that applied to me. I talked to Sean Yates, the British guy who was then one of our directeurs sportifs at Tinkoff about the issues he'd been through at Sky when Mark Cavendish and Bradley Wiggins were hunting the green and yellow jerseys respectively. We agreed that this was a different situation, as Mark rides as the spearhead of a team effort and expects assistance, lead-out trains, breaks being chased down, tows back to the main group, dedicated domestiques, all things that are difficult for a team to provide when they are protecting the interests of a genuine G.C. contender or race leader at the same time.

I didn't want any help at all. I just wanted to be left alone to do my thing. I didn't need anybody to help me. And that left seven other guys free to do anything Alberto wanted. It seemed to me that if we couldn't win the Tour with seven highly paid hand-picked domestiques, we weren't likely to do much better with eight. It was hardly likely to be my fault.

"No," said Feltrin, "We'll need your strength in the first week to hold things together."

"I need to race from stage 1, or the green is gone," I explained. The points competition is so loaded toward the rough and tumble of the first few days that anybody coming late to the party has no chance of leaving with the spoils. "I don't need any help, Stefano; just let me get on with it. You've got seven other guys. OK, if Alberto and I are the only riders in the front group, of course I will help. But if seven guys can't pace him back up after a puncture or a crash, eight guys won't be able to do it either."

"We can't risk it. You might crash in a sprint."

"Oh, Stefano, I know you've never ridden the Tour, but have you ever even seen one? I don't need a sprint to crash. I can crash anywhere."

To his credit, Alberto never put any pressure on me to be his bodyguard around France. As we were all preparing for the Dutch start in Utrecht, I found a moment to speak to him alone. There was a stage after the weekend that went through the Badlands south of Lille, hitting no fewer than seven secteurs of Paris–Roubaix cobbles. I knew it was somewhere that my experience could make a difference if he needed it.

"Listen, Alberto, stage 4, the pavé. I'll be there with you. Don't worry."

"Thank you, Peter."

That was it.

In more general terms, there is a much greater danger of internal team rivalry when you have two riders going for the same thing. It was before my time, but people still talk about the epic battle between Bernard Hinault and Greg LeMond when they were on the same La Vie Claire team at the 1986 Tour. Less obvious, but another problem for Yates to sort out in that Sky team of 2012 was the battle between Wiggins and Froome. Two riders trying to occupy the same space in the team, in the race, and even on the mountain, raises issues for even the strongest squads, and it's nearly always when the climbing starts. I should point out that for all these so-called problems, both La Vie Claire and Sky won those races and gave the fans enough entertainment that we're still talking about both races today. Why so serious?

———

I'm trying to tell you things in the order they happened, but sometimes everything happens at once.

We were in Utrecht getting ready for the Tour. It was the Wednesday before the kick-off on Saturday. Oleg phoned me up and said, "Peter, we need to talk about your contract."

Still convinced I would be retiring at the first available opportunity, I was worried he was going to ask me to extend my contract on the back of my recent run of victories, or make sure I knew it was cast iron, as a lot of business gets discussed at the Tour de France and a lot of deals are done for new teams and transfers.

"OK, Oleg, what's on your mind?" I answered nervously.

"We need to renegotiate it."

"In what way?"

"We need to reduce it."

This was a surprise. I didn't think I could be surprised any more. My life has been full of surprises, and I thought I was fairly unshockable, but I admit my stomach flipped.

"Erm . . . why, Oleg?"

"Listen, Peter, I brought you to the team to win me some classics. I've got Tour riders, and that's been great. But this year I've taken you on because I need Monument wins; that's what I'm paying you for. And you were shit at the classics."

I took a deep breath. I could see what he was saying, but in a race with one hundred different stories, anything can happen, and I don't remember there being any suggestion of my salary being performance related. OK, sometimes a sponsor might give you a bonus if you did something extra special, but I haven't heard of them withholding pay because you tried your best but didn't cross the line first.

"Yes, I agree, I was shit. But everybody knows why: Bjarne, Bobby, overtraining, contract negotiations, virus . . . I've come back stronger. I've got 10 wins and jerseys for Team Tinkoff already."

"Yes, they're lovely, thanks, but I didn't sign you because I wanted a points jersey in the Tour of fucking Switzerland. I want a Roubaix, a Flanders, a Primavera, or at the very least a Gent–Wevelgem or an Amstel Gold. So, basically, you owe me your March and April salary."

"Oh, man. Seriously?"

"Look, I know you're getting ready for the Tour de France, so I'll leave you to prepare, I'll think about it for a few days, then I'll call Giovanni."

"OK. Bye, Oleg."

"Ciao, Peter, good to talk to you."

Classic Oleg.

I called Giovanni, and we had a Team Peter powwow. Giovanni began to shuffle some legal arguments and go through the contract again just to make sure there were no loopholes for Oleg to exploit. We agreed that we should just keep our heads down and say nothing to anyone as it might just blow over. No reaction, no press, no response.

On the Saturday morning, with the first stage time trial that afternoon, Oleg came over and found me by the bus getting ready.

"Hi Peter, how are the legs?"

"Good, thanks, Boss."

"Listen, that stuff the other day about the contract? Just forget about it OK; it's all good."

"Oh. OK. Thanks again. I won't let you down."

"I know, I know. And all this stuff about team instructions and riding like a domestique for Alberto? Fuck 'em. Fuck 'em all. Get me that green jersey."

You had to laugh. Oleg Tinkov, what a character. But it did underline a serious point that never disappeared the whole time I was on the team: Who should I listen to? Who did I need to please?

―――――

That was the race of second places. After the time trial—it was too long to be called a prologue, they decided—there was a flat stage across the reclaimed lands that give the Netherlands its name, finishing on an island. I knew there would be crosswinds, and, bizarrely, the predictions about helping Alberto came true, as we were both alert enough to make sure we were in the front split. It was a good day for the team, who smashed it hard on the front in lashing rain and gale-force winds, and also for Sky, and we drove it between us for Alberto and Froome. By the finish, Quintana and Nibali had lost a minute, and I felt free to contest the sprint. It was a tight one, going to a photo, but Andre Greipel's tire touched the line before mine, and I had my first second place.

After guiding Alberto over the pavé as promised with plenty of effort but no real incident, I finished second in the sprint again, this time to John Degenkolb, who was having an incredible season, winning both Milan–San Remo and then Paris–Roubaix on these same cobbles. Unfortunately for both of us, we were only sprinting for second place on the stage, as Tony Martin had clipped off the front of the hard-core group that remained in contention with a few kilometers to go, and we just couldn't catch him. He took the stage and the yellow jersey with it. Another near miss for me, but I wasn't worried. The chances would come.

Like the next day, when I was second to Andre Greipel again.

And the next day, when I was second to Zdeněk Štybar.

Actually, that one really hurt. Well, it didn't hurt me as badly as it hurt Tony Martin, who was in a crash within sight of the line.

The yellow jersey has no more padding than any other, and it couldn't prevent his collarbone from cracking, leaving his heart as broken as his clavicle. Of course, I didn't know he was hurt at the time; there was just a mess of riders everywhere and a chance to win a stage. But first we had to catch Štybar, who'd jumped himself into a handy lead just as the Lycra hit the tarmac. Well before that day and continuing to this, whenever there's chasing to be done, it seems everybody looks at me. Seriously? I still don't really get it. It had already been demonstrated on a few painful occasions in this race that there were other sprinters capable of beating me, and they had powerful teams to help them. But no, let's wait and let Sagan chase. I was beginning to get a bit fed up, so I sat up and invited somebody else to chase Štybar. There were only a few hundred meters to go: If we didn't get together and chase together, he would win. We didn't. He did. And guess what? Yes, I was second. I was thinking of getting a new jersey made. Most second places. The brown jersey, maybe.

I wasn't second the next day. I was third. Second loser, I suppose. To make up for it, I found myself second in the G.C., so I could keep my imaginary brown jersey.

Second in the sprint again the next day, stage 8, to Alejandro Valverde on the slopes of the Mur-de-Bretagne, but we were both outdone by two late attackers anyway. At least I was consistent, I suppose, but it was getting pretty frustrating. By consolation, that consistency meant that I wouldn't have to wear my notional brown jersey the following day, as I'd nicked enough points off Greipel to get my favorite Robin Hood–colored jersey back. Rob the rich to give to the poor? The way things were going, I bet if I ran the Sheriff of Nottingham's coach off the road, I'd get to the treasure chest and find Greipel or Cav had already helped themselves.

A week went past. We did a team time trial. We climbed the Pyrenees. I slipped out of the top 10, unsurprisingly, but I still had the green jersey. For a while, I'd also held the white jersey of best young rider overall. Some people found it hard to believe that I still qualified for this, and sometimes I felt like one of them. It was hard to believe that I was still only 25. Still, I was all burnt out and washed up, wasn't I? So that white jersey must have been mystifying. Thankfully, I didn't have to wear it seeing as I had the green one or people would have been mightily confused. When we got into the mountains, I lost it to Nairo Quintana, which must have been even more mind-blowing for the public, as he looks much older than 25.

Alberto lost some time. Rafal Majka won a stage for us, but we were all in shock. Feeling unwell for the first week of the race, our universally loved and respected captain, Ivan Basso, went for some tests on the rest day. He was hit with the completely paralyzing news that he had testicular cancer and needed immediate treatment. Within days, he was having surgery in Italy.

Ivan had been a part of my life since turning pro, as my team leader and a double Giro d'Italia winner at Liquigas, and now as a hugely experienced skipper for Alberto here at Tinkoff. We didn't often ride the same races, but his relentless positivity, smile, and time for everyone he meets had a huge effect on me, as I'm sure they have for all his former teammates. Off the bike, we shared Giovanni as an agent, so I had come to know him and look up to him more than most. Nobody knew what to say as the news came through, and the team felt that weight of events bigger than cycling begin to descend upon us.

As a postscript, Ivan made a full recovery from his illness but, at 37, he felt it was time to wrap up his long career. He is not lost to the world of cycling, however, and it is a racing certainty that he will continue to play major roles in the future of our sport.

At the time though, you can imagine the news was devastating, and it was hard to focus. All any of us could do was to concentrate on our own internal commitments to the race and do the best we could without him, and for him.

After a week of being in the bunch, I was beginning to think about taking the green jersey to Paris and maybe winning a stage in it at last. So it was almost comforting to come second again on stage 13, this time to Greg Van Avermaet.

On stage 16, fed up with losing sprint stages, I tried my luck on a mountain stage. There were two second-category climbs on it. Second? That sounded like my kind of category, and it had a downhill plunge to the finish in gap in the Alps, which I thought would suit me.

I came in second.

There was one stage for sprinters left, the glorious pageant of a gallop up the Champs-Elysées and a hero's welcome in Paris for the winner. I was determined not to come second. I didn't. I came in seventh.

On Family

Did you know that Jerusalem artichokes aren't artichokes at all? And that they don't come from Jerusalem either? Amazing, no? They are actually very tall plants that look like sunflowers, but have a large, gnarly tuber in their roots that looks like a big, long piece of fresh ginger that you might pick up in a more enlightened supermarket. "What about the Jerusalem bit?" I hear you cry. Well, it seems English-speaking settlers in the New World misunderstood their French-speaking counterparts when they described a sunflower as a "girasol" and the name was born.

And if you think I had to look that up, then maybe I did, just to check, but it saved you doing it, didn't it?

Another, more accurate name for a Jerusalem artichoke is a sunroot, and this is where this whole baffling section might start to make a bit more sense. My wife, Katarina, has started a company with her father called Sunroot. It's a range of gluten-free, zero-fat foods all based around a core foodstuff made from Jerusalem artichokes. The plant is grown and harvested widely in Slovakia, so it's an effective enterprise to boost the local economy, make something genuinely useful, and give Katarina an outlet for her creative and business-minded brain. They do all sorts of stuff: hot chocolate powder, blueberry jam, yogurt-coated snacks, white-chocolate-coated fruit drops . . . But the most useful thing is a flour that you can use for all your usual baking. Sunroot also has the benefit of being naturally sweet, so it doesn't need sugar added to it in a lot of recipes. Cakes without getting fat. Yes!

The other thing sunroot does is grow like wildfire, so much so that it can take over if you don't keep an eye on it, a bit like rhododendron does in parts of Europe. Like rhododendron, it looks pretty, so people don't clear it. This got up the nose of one particular Slovak politician to such a degree that he got a law passed to have it banned. Can you see a pattern emerging here? Naturally, that would have been Katarina's business down the drain without a backward glance, but fortunately there are a lot of farmers, growers, and sellers of sunroot in Slovakia, so he eventually backed down. The politician probably proposed the law because his neighbor's garden was overgrown. As you know by now, that's how things tend to work over in Slovakia.

If you put "Jerusalem artichoke" into Google, you'll get the description I gave you at the top of this chapter. If you put "sunroot" into Google, there's a good chance you'll get Katarina and me pretending to be Olivia Newton John and John Travolta as Sandy and Danny in *Grease*. We did it as a promotional thing for Sunroot, but we also did it for a laugh. Why so serious? We've always had silly ideas. One of the benefits of being UCI World Champion is that you can get away with doing them. Actually, that's not quite right . . . we still would have done it, but doing our own private lip sync battle in the kitchen isn't quite as much fun as getting a crew in to recreate the fairground set for "You're the One That I Want" and getting it edited shot-by-shot to match the original.

Katarina and I met at my house in Žilina. Actually, let me backtrack a little bit. When Juraj and I managed to start getting paid to ride bikes and when we weren't at the Liquigas flat in Italy, we found ourselves a house in between the motorway and the huge bend in the River Vah as it widens into the Hricov Lake. They started building a bridge across it there shortly before we got the house. I was there recently, and they've just finished the bridge 10 years on. I love Slovakia, but it makes me smile.

I had the bit of land that adjoined it too, and I was starting to earn a bit more money. I had a couple of cars by then, so I thought I'd build a garage for them on this land. That's all. Then I thought

I might like my own place to sleep, so it should have a bedroom above the cars. That's all I'd need. Then, often when I come back to Slovakia, I'll have a friend traveling with me, so I should get a guest room. That'd be enough. But then, if I was back in the winter, which can be pretty dark and cold in Žilina, I might want a gym and a sauna in the loft to keep fit. That's all a man needs.

In the end, the whole project morphed completely, and we ended up not building a house for ourselves at all. Instead it became the basis for the sports center I'd been trying to establish. Young Slovakian athletes from all different sports can go there to live, train, and generally get the support they need to make the step from keen youngster to full-time athlete.

But before we knew that would happen, Juraj and I put out a request for a few local companies to quote on doing the building. One guy I particularly liked ran a little construction company with his father, and they seemed pretty well organized. After meeting them in the winter of 2012, I went off for my first concerted crack at the classics and came back with a fifth, fourth, third, and second place to my name. The third was at Amstel Gold in Holland, after which Juraj and I had a spring barbecue party at our place to celebrate. As it was next to the plot where this garage/bachelor pad would be going up, I invited the construction guy to the party to hang out with us and talk about the project. He turned up with this girl who instantly made a bit of an impression on me: tall, beautiful, but with a confident way about her that seemed to suggest there was more to her world than a construction company in Žilina. I was just thinking that he was a lucky bastard, when he introduced her as his sister. Happy days.

Things didn't happen between us immediately, but I texted her a few times, and she texted back, and before too long, people started to realize that we were seeing each other.

Katarina—you'd worked that out I hope—was very well traveled, having worked for DHL, and she had lived in Australia. She had friends everywhere: Belgium, Holland, the Czech Republic, Poland. Wherever I went, she seemed to know someone, so after a while I said: "If you think you might want to be with me, come and see my life. Come and see what it's like."

It was a great time. In 2013 I had my best spring so far, picking up my first classic at Gent–Wevelgem and my first Monument podiums with second places at Milan–San Remo and the Tour of Flanders. Traveling with Katarina shone a new light on everything, and I felt stronger for having her point of view and support alongside me.

The problem was the problem that all of us face at some point: time. Some of us have not enough, some too much. At that point, it was certainly the former, with the training, racing, commercial responsibilities, family, friends, and girlfriend all deserving a bigger chunk of my attention than they were getting. We started picking races to go to together, so we could enjoy a bit more: no quick turnarounds, no training camps, no long transfers. The Tour of California was a perfect place for us, providing the chilled-out lifestyle we both wanted. We could carry on and be together at a relaxed, personal altitude training camp in Utah or Tahoe. The Tour Down Under is a great place to go, too, and usually the world championships is as well as you're in the same place for a few days and in the more informal atmosphere of the national team rather than a sponsored outfit with professional demands.

We decided that the classics would be too much. Maybe, say, Paris–Roubaix, or Flanders, but to do the whole period together would be too intense. The same thing goes for the Tour de France. A stage here or there is fun and something to look forward to in the middle of the madness of the Tour, but you get dragged into the routine grind if you do it all the time, and that's no good for either of us.

There's also the team and my teammates to think of. Togetherness is important in any team in any sport. At some point, you'll need to rely on each other, and the unique pro-cycling system of first among equals will be put to the test. There wasn't room on the Tour, for instance, for nine riders to bring their families along for the ride, let alone the directors', mechanics', and soigneurs' families. Plus, much of the communication and planning at big races takes place when you sit around the breakfast table or dinner table. Big team training camps were not ideal places for us to go together for those reasons, too.

I also realized that, more and more, I needed a sanctuary in my life. Somewhere that specifically wasn't a bike race or a sponsor event or a training camp every once in a while. When I get back to our apartment in Monaco after a grueling series of races or a convoluted travel plan, the weight just lifts from my shoulders when I see Katarina there.

The world outside cycling has become even more insane for me lately, due to four different things. The first three are the rainbow jerseys I brought home from America, the Middle East, and Scandinavia. The fourth is the most wonderful thing that ever happened to me, and his name is Marlon. The first three have incrementally heaped more attention on our little family, especially in Slovakia, where, as I have said before, we are a young country short on national heroes. Having a world champion in any sport is something we're not used to, and getting one in a global sport like cycling three years running is understandably a big deal for us, but when they run out of things to write about me, they just make stuff up. It's pretty irritating.

These days, back in Slovakia, if I want to go out with friends for a few beers at a nightclub, everyone will tell me that we'll have to have the club closed just for us because once word gets around, everybody will be piling into the club and piling over to us for pictures, autographs, a chat, all sorts of things. I don't mind that, I always try to be polite, and I genuinely can't remember a time that I've turned down requests for selfies and autographs, but sometimes you just want to relax with friends, you know? It also means being on your best behavior 24/7 or you'll wake up the next morning and see an awful photo of yourself looking worse for wear at three in the morning. Of course, this rule doesn't apply to the people who want to join you at that time of night, and the later it gets, the drunker they tend to be, and the more awkward the situation. To be honest with you, it ends up that you just don't go out.

It's the same when Katarina and I go out for a meal. You usually like to do that kind of thing when you've been apart for a little while, just to relax together, catch up on what's been happening in the worlds that we share but sometimes only overlap. Once again, there will be requests for signatures and photographs with us, which is fine; people tend to be a lot more polite and respectful in a restaurant than in a bar or club. It gets more difficult when you're trying to talk about what you've been doing, who's been doing what, or maybe make plans for the coming days and weeks, and you feel people's ears on neighboring tables pricking up and sense them leaning in a bit closer, hoping to pick up a nugget of information. Once again, you end up eating at home.

Marlon has just focused my resolve to keep my family safe from that. I'm not planning on any celebrity magazine spreads of our home life, pictures of him in the latest toddler fashions on the news, or scenes of him in his school uniform with paparazzi outside the school gates on his first day.

Monaco helps. I was talking to a friend from London the other day about living in Richmond—yes, the London Richmond—and he was talking about seeing Mick Jagger in the pub or Pete Townshend in the supermarket and people not really taking any notice. That's the Monaco effect. I'm small fry here when you're living alongside Lewis Hamilton and Ringo Starr. Residents are used to seeing recognizable faces around and tend not to get so excited.

I think that when it's time for him to go to school here, Marlon will find it easier to fit in and not get hassled. It's very international, and everybody is treated respectfully and similarly. French schools—the Monegasque system adopts French education—have a great reputation for instilling good self-esteem and respect for others, while letting kids find their own way.

I think that's what this is about, to be honest, letting Marlon find his own path. If we can protect him from too much aggravation until he's old enough to make his own choices about what he wants to do, what he wants to be, who he wants to hang out with, then we'll have done OK. I don't want him wrapped up in cotton wool his whole life; I just want to buy him some space, time, and freedom if I can. And if he wants to be a cyclist? Well, yes, riding a bike is fun, but I think there are easier ways to earn a few euros.

————

Growing up, there was nothing that my parents wouldn't do for any of us: Milan, the eldest; the middle one, Juraj; my sister, Daniela; or me, the baby of the family and spoiled by everybody. I have my mum to thank for the incredible sacrifices she had to make in order to raise four children. Thanks to her we were fed, educated, and raised as adults with big hearts and an important sense of principle. While we weren't by any means well-off, we didn't want for anything because our welfare was so evidently her main concern. There's no doubt that when I'm praised for actions off the bike, it is Mum who must take the credit.

It was my dad, L'ubomír, who buttoned back his protective instincts and encouraged me to venture forth into the great outdoors. He would always be there and wanted full reports on everything we'd done. When Juraj and I started racing, he loaded everything we needed in the family car and shuttled us round the country. Then out of the country . . . the Czech Republic, Poland, Croatia, even Germany. The packed car really made for quite a scene—kit, clothes, food, bikes on the roof, and then somehow Juraj and I would be wedged in among it all. It might not have been the most comfortable, but it was an adventure every weekend. I never questioned how we could afford it or what plans and dreams he had of his own. He was still a young man.

I remember going to a mountain bike race somewhere in Europe, and there was this incredible downhill course with enormous jumps and breathtaking drop-offs. I was desperate to have a go on it, but Dad said no. That was pretty rare, so I listened and didn't sulk too much.

My oldest brother, Milan, was my hero. He still is. He knew everything, knew everyone, could do anything, could go anywhere. You just knew that Milan would do all right in this world. He was just like a younger version of my dad: confident without being cocky, popular with everyone, but always with a bit of mischief in him. He also made a valuable contribution to my early career decision-making. Back in the day, when I was first offered a place on the Liquigas squad, it wasn't a given that I'd accept. It's funny to think back now, but the very idea was really quite terrifying. Remember, I was still a young man, a boy really, and joining Liquigas meant leaving home, my family, and friends and moving to Italy, an unfamiliar country where I couldn't speak a word of the local language. No, I'd be much better off staying in the comfort of Slovakia. There'd be other opportunities, no doubt.

Milan got wind of this and took me to one side.

"I hear you're thinking about staying put?"

I nodded.

"You want my advice?"

Of course I did. He was the wise big brother that I looked up to.

He slapped me in the face and said, "Go pack your things and get yourself to Italy. This is the best opportunity you'll ever get in your life. If you turn it down, you'll regret it forever."

Needless to say, he was right then, and he's right now.

When I went back to Slovakia recently, we spent the day together. I had some business to sort out, and Milan came to all the banks and offices with me. By the time I'd wrapped up all the necessary errands, I didn't want to leave, and it seemed he didn't want me to go either. In the end, he jumped in the car with us and started heading back from Žilina to the airport in Bratislava, even though that was doubtless going to leave him stranded in the middle of nowhere. Gabri was stressing because we had to catch a flight, and we had an English journalist with us. Milan and I made Gabri stop at every single service station on the motorway.

"Gabri, I need a piss."

"Gabri, I'm thirsty."

"Gabri, I'm hungry."

"Gabri, I need another piss."

We went into a garage and bought some beers, shaking one up for a couple of strenuous minutes, before handing it generously to the journalist when we got back in the car.

"Gabri, we need to stop again; this guy is soaking wet."

In the end, Milan left us at a garage and phoned a friend for a lift back to Žilina. He's the sort of guy who will always have a friend to do that.

That morning, I'd taken Gabri to see my sister, Daniela. She's gorgeous, the greatest sister in the world, and Slovakia's best hairdresser—the reason for the visit. He was due a trim and loved how she'd styled his hair last time round. I left strict instructions for Daniela before Milan and I headed off.

When we got back Gabri was sulking and wearing a hat. I turned to Daniela: "Did everything go to plan?"

"Yes. I cut it nice, just as you said. Showed him how he looked in the mirror. He was very pleased. Then I shaved it all off, just like you said."

———

Another person in Slovakia I miss hugely is my friend Martin. One night we were out in a club. It must have been when I was first winning races because fellow partygoers were coming up to me for an autograph. I was obliging and good-natured and did all of them, while Martin was constantly taking the piss. "Don't you want my signature, Peter?" he asked. I called his bluff, pulled down my trousers, and he signed my thigh with a marker.

When I returned later that year, we went out again, and I said, "Hey, Martin, check this out," and dropped my trousers again. He was stunned to see his autograph still clearly displayed on my thigh, months later. How come? I'd had it tattooed on. He nearly passed out.

I thought I'd got one over on him for all time. But when I went home around Christmas after winning my first UCI World Championship in Richmond, he trumped me in a way I don't think I can ever beat. Martin took off his shirt and turned around. Across his back was a whole panorama shot in full glorious color of me in my Slovakia kit, giving the victory salute as I won the title. It was my turn to be speechless.

I had to get another tattoo after my first one because, according to the Italians, one tattoo is unlucky. But then, they are a superstitious bunch. I've been on my way to a race with Italian teammates when they've seen a black cat, stopped, turned around, and gone a much longer way round. If you're at dinner and they ask you for the salt, you have to put it down for them to pick up, rather than handing it to them. Weird stuff like that.

Anyway, I got another one. It's the Heath Ledger version of the Joker with a bit of me thrown in. And what's he saying? Can't you guess? Why so serious?

Then I got my world championship victories added to my side, so that little list is longer than I'd ever expected. But my favorite shows my fist touching Marlon's tiny fist when he was really little. It's lovely. So, depending on whether you count my world's tattoo as one or three, I've either got four or six. Who knows what might be next?

AUTUMN

Remember how I mentioned that I enjoy a personal challenge from a friend, or sometimes a little wager, to inject a touch of motivation to a particular race or task expected of me? Now, you might suggest, very reasonably, that a man from a modest background with a very short career window being paid a decent amount of money to win bike races should need no further reward, and you'd be right. The only trouble is that all sounds a bit serious, and you already know where I stand on being too serious. This enables me to focus and really go for it, but still keep it fun.

There have been various dares, bets, and trades over the years among the members of Team Peter, but one of the first that sticks in my mind is the bet I made with Giovanni before going to Richmond for the 2015 world's.

"No, wait ..." Giovanni steps in to remind me. "What about Liquigas at your first Tour de France?"

Ah, yes. Giovanni got into one of our whadaya-gonna-do-for-me-if-I-win? conversations with the boss of Liquigas, Paolo Zani, before my first Tour in 2012.

"I said that if Peter can win two stages for Liquigas at his first Tour, it would be a remarkable achievement and that they should mark it in an appropriate way . . . maybe with a car, for instance? Presidente Zani said, 'OK, let's make it two stages and a green jersey.' And then he'd give Peter a Porsche."

And what happened, Lomba?

"You won three stages. And the green jersey."

Bang. So now I can tell you what I had in mind for Richmond in 2015. Beforehand, I'd been back to altitude to get some relaxed miles in. We'd hit upon a very attractive plan of staying on the western side of the Atlantic after the Tour, mixing a bit of rest and relaxation with altitude training in August, then building up to the race in September. We knew it was a balancing act to hold my condition from the Tour, which was really good, and to keep me free from anxiety and fatigue, which had been as bad in the spring as my fitness was good in the summer. We were also trying to manage a problem with my hip (that I still have to keep an eye on now and will do for the rest of my career, maybe my life). I'm naturally a bit twisted on the bike, and that period of overtraining in the spring had really made my right hip and lower back tight. Maroš was working on it right through the year, and I was doing some gym work to improve my core strength and stability. It really assists with my climbing and big efforts, especially increasing power when you want to stay in the saddle, over the cobbles, for instance. My routine in the gym after training keeps me strong and injury free.

This time, we headed to Lake Tahoe in California. The lake is at around 6,200 feet and surrounded by such beautiful mountains that you can't help but feel relaxed and happy. Giovanni, Katarina, and I were having dinner, a really pleasant meal, talking about the spring, about my hip, how I was feeling, and about motivation for Richmond. Now, as I said, Lomba was a shit-hot rider in his day. We didn't cross over, but my coach now, Sylwester Szmyd, was in the pro peloton alongside him for a few seasons. There was a string of strong Italian "horses," like Giovanni, Martinelli, Scirea, and Poli, unsung heroes who their whole team could rely on to do the work of three men each, but also to watch carefully as they could keep you out of trouble. "Foxes" is how Sylwester described these guys, and I would suggest that smartness and a nose for a solution have been very useful to Giovanni (and me, by implication) after he retired and set up his agency. However, unlike a lot of modern ex-riders who stay in the business, Lomba hung up his wheels for the last time at his last race, and they have gathered dust in his garage ever since. Either that or he made a killing on eBay—that's probably more his style. The point is that unlike people like Patxi or Sean Yates, both awesome directors and coaches for me at that time at Tinkoff, I've never ridden a bike with Giovanni. Sean Yates still races against his sons and his brothers in England sometimes. But not Giovanni.

So, when he cracked open a very nice bottle of wine in Tahoe, we were celebrating, but planning too. My hip was feeling great after concerted strengthening and manipulation by the genius Maroš, despite the team doctors having declared that I would need an operation. The wine was called No. 1, and Giovanni asked what could he do to repay me if I finished No. 1 in Richmond.

I thought about it. Thought about the glorious 120-kilometer rolling route I had ridden all the way around Lake Tahoe that morning. "Lomba, if I become UCI World Champion, you are going to come back here and ride a lap of the lake with me."

He thought long and hard. One thing about Giovanni is that he never just says, "Yes." He always has to twist it, or add a clause, or make it more interesting.

"OK," he said at last, turning to Katarina, "but you're coming too."

The three of us raised our glasses. The game was on.

———

I went to the Vuelta a España in the autumn, mainly to pick up a little form for the world's but also to try to remember what it was like to win. Fortunately, it came to me early when I outsprinted John Degenkolb and Nacer Bouhanni to grab a stage and a spell in the points jersey early on, no mean feat in a race as mountainous and explosive as the Tour of Spain. Unfortunately, my luck didn't hold far beyond the first week, when some fool on a neutral service motorcycle whizzed up the side of the bunch and knocked me off toward the end of stage 8. With some deep bruising and a certain amount of Slovakian skin lost to Murcian tarmac, I was forced to withdraw from the race. If that wasn't enough to put my nose out of joint, I then learned the race had fined me for throwing my bike on the ground and kicking a race car in frustration in the aftermath of the crash. Thanks, guys. You might as well pop up to the hospital while you're at it and see if you can extract some penalties from old ladies who have sworn at muggers while having their handbags stolen.

Sometimes it's hard to stick to your aim of always taking a positive from a negative, but on this occasion two good things came about indirectly. First, eight days of racing was good time to get in the bank before the almost daily mountaintop finishes that characterize the Vuelta truly kicked in, meaning that at least I wasn't going to finish the race tired. I could focus fully on Richmond.

Top: One thing that has accompanied all of my UCI World Championship victories is the incredible forest of Slovak flags. It doesn't feel like I come from a small country any more.

Middle top: I was surprised to be able to even start in Bergen after being ill, and the objective for the majority of the 276.5 km race was to last as long as I could.

Middle bottom: Some sprints are explosive, some are slow burners, but few are as intense for such a prolonged effort as the world's were in Bergen. If the course had been 50 cm shorter, I would just be a double world champion.

Bottom: If anybody questioned my astonishment at winning my third consecutive world's, they only had to see my face on the podium. Alexander Kristoff (L) and Michael Matthews (R) joined me on the podium.

Top left: This fellow looks barely old enough to be out of school, let alone riding a bike professionally.

Middle left: My third Tour stage win on debut in Metz in front of Andre Greipel and, of course, another quirky Tour de France victory salute.

Bottom: Riding into Paris at the denouement of my first Tour de France in the green points classification jersey alongside best young rider Tejay van Garderen, race winner Bradley Wiggins, and King of the Mountains Thomas Voeckler was an experience to savor. I wanted more.

Top right: Lining up with Liquigas teammates and Italian legends Ivan Basso and Vincenzo Nibali for my first Tour de France start in Liège.

Middle right: All his years of driving around Europe to support my early career finally paid off. 2012 was a very happy year for my father, L'ubomír.

Top left: The first hero of Slovak cycling, Ján Valach, seen here in 1989 at the height of his professional career. He is still inspiring me from behind the wheel at BORA-hansgrohe.

Bottom: Adding my support to kids events like this one in my home town of Žilina led to the formation of the Peter Sagan Academy, established to develop young talent.

Top right: Being an outdoorsy kind of kid, playing every conceivable sport, was hugely influential on my career. I love getting new generations of Slovak children out in the open air, such as at this Kids Tour event in 2015.

Top left: My first move as a professional was to the headline-grabbing Tinkoff team and a new coach in Bobby Julich.

Bottom left: There was never a dull moment when Oleg Tinkov was around. Here he is in 2015, testing the seams of my fourth Tour de France green jersey and my first for Team Tinkoff.

Top right: The driving force behind my arrival at Tinkoff was the team's founder, Bjarne Riis.

Bottom right: If you wanted to be entertained, charmed, amused, or offended, Oleg was always on hand.

Top left: Conflict at the top of the Tinkoff organization between Stefano Feltrin, Oleg Tinkov, and Bjarne Riis ultimately cost Riis his job.

Bottom: My second year at Tinkoff was far less turbulent than the first.

Top right: Much was made of the supposed rivalry for team leadership at Tinkoff between Alberto Contador and myself, but neither of us saw it as an issue. We had an easy friendship and mutual respect.

Top left: The Tinkoff team time trial squad at the 2015 UCI World Championships in Richmond, Virginia, may look pretty cool, but that was a day none of us will want to remember. Everything that could go wrong, did.

Top right: The tricky circuit in Virginia suited me perfectly. The nature of circuit racing means you can hone your line into the corners on every lap, something that paid dividends for me that day.

Middle: The moment when I finally realized that no, they weren't going to catch me. I was going to be the UCI World Champion.

Bottom: Time enough to actually enjoy the last few yards and get used to the idea of wearing the UCI rainbow jersey.

Top left: What do you think? I could get used to wearing this, I reckon.

Top right: Michal Kolář, my brother, Juraj, and my dad, L'ubomír . . . at this point it was still sinking in for all of us.

Middle: It's nice to be thrown in the air by your team, and even nicer to be caught, but I am acutely aware of the Slovakia team's unquestioning commitment. It was an amazing day for all of us.

Bottom: Flying the flag for my country.

Top: Receiving congratulations from Tom Boonen after winning Gent–Wevelgem in 2016.

Middle top: I quickly became very familiar with the concept that if something can be manufactured, it can be manufactured with a rainbow on it.

Middle bottom: Breaking my Monument slump with a hugely satisfying solo win at the 2016 Tour of Flanders and paying due respect to the jersey by putting it on the top step of one of the greatest podiums in pro cycling.

Bottom: Accepting congratulations from the one and only Fabian Cancellara. How many times had this scene been shot the opposite way around?

And that was by no means the first time that season that motos had got in the way of the race they were supposed to be assisting. The most common issue is that as the race compresses toward the finish and the pace picks up, the support guys who have been following the race for any number of reasons have to squeeze past and get to the finish before the race does, leading to some risk-taking, bad decisions, dangerous moments, and occasionally crashes like mine. I'm pleased to say there's been some genuine improvements made since then, the simplest and most useful being improved deviation shortcuts for traffic to leave the race route and breeze to the finish without having to use the same route as the race.

I got to Virginia a little bit earlier than I probably would have liked in preparation for the road race, especially with concerns about that Vuelta tumble still so fresh. But an event that was introduced into the UCI World Championships in 2012 is the team time trial, which we race in with our usual professional teams, not national teams.

You can imagine that Oleg would love a world title with "Tink-off" emblazoned on it. Not Contador, Meika, or Sagan of Tinkoff, but just Tinkoff. Winners. Champions.

And so a week before the road race took place, I was on the line with five strong Tinkoff teammates, focused on a medal that would mean that I would have something to bring back from the other side of the Atlantic, no matter what happened the following weekend.

Manuele Boaro was a bit of a horse for us, an Italian TT specialist who had ridden smoothly and strongly in these events as a powerful teammate on a number of occasions, so when his saddle slipped down after only 3 kilometers and the rest of us sailed off into the distance, it was a massive blow. We weren't just losing a rider of his quality very early, but the world's TTT is a six-man event, unlike the nine teammates who gather together in the Grand Tours. That meant that instead of each of us doing 16 percent of the work, we would have to do 20 percent for virtually the whole 40 kilometers or so we had to cover. That was bound to be a factor in the closing stages.

Well, it should have been, but it wasn't. But not for a good reason.

The remaining five of us were pulling pretty hard, and the changes were good—very tight and close. Too tight and close, it turned out. Michael Valgren was in the line behind Michael Rogers and managed to get his front wheel just marginally alongside the Australian's rear wheel, and that was it. Crunch. Both of them went down, Rogers straight over the bars, and Valgren skidding along the tarmac on his shoulder and arse. It wasn't pretty.

For a moment, Maciej Bodnar and I sat up, still rolling, and looked at each other. What do we do? Push on? But the rules for the world TTT are strict: The time is taken when the fourth rider crosses the line. Not much point in me, Body, and Christopher Juul-Jensen racing to the line and leaving our stricken teammates behind. We weren't even sure they'd be able to continue, but both the Michaels are tough guys, and they had that added incentive of neither wanting to be the one who let the team down. Leaving Lycra, skin, and blood on the tarmac, we gingerly regrouped. By that time, Boaro and his fixed bike had got back up to us too, so we rode on as a sextet, but now in search of nothing more than dignity and obligation to each other and the team. Being the senior riders who hadn't had any problems, Body and I pulled for most of it, so I guess it was training that wouldn't go amiss. Nobody was cheering at the finish when we arrived stone-cold last of 27, eight minutes and more behind gold medalists BMC. Inauspicious. Thank goodness we hadn't set off last. They'd probably have packed everything up by the time we arrived.

A week later, the men's road race of the 2015 UCI World Championships was held on a lovely late summer's day on the eastern seaboard of America. Richmond, one of the oldest settlements in the whole union, was named after leafy Richmond-upon-Thames on the outskirts of London, by pioneers of the Jamestown settlement. The state, Virginia, was named in honor of the first Queen Elizabeth of England by the great explorer Walter

Raleigh. Pocahontas and George Washington called this part of the world home. There's a sense of history in Richmond, Virginia, that is rarely found in the United States, and the Virginians guard it fiercely, as you might expect.

What can I say? I was there all week, you pick this stuff up.

One of their nods to the past is found in the neat cobbles that line some of the roads. The locals might have been proud of their streets, but I was pretty keen on them too.

I really liked the circuit. Really liked it. There were 2 twisting kilometers of intense climbing, descending, and cornering, then a relaxing circuit where you could take stock, get your breath back, see what damage had been done, a climb, then the intense section would be on you once more. The damage was nearly done extraordinarily early. With a slightly longer first lap being followed by 15 laps of 16 kilometers each, I was settling in for the long haul, proudly wearing the blue, white, and red of Slovakia alongside Juraj and Michal Kolář, and happy to be there and considered a "player." This player was very nearly back in the changing rooms before the game had even properly begun. The race director withdrew his flag into the leading car to signify that the neutralized section was done and the race was on, and the pace went stratospheric in an instant. Now, this is very common in Grand Tours these days, but a race as long as the world's, ridden by national squads rather than teams with commercial

TV exposure in mind, tends to be a little more thoughtful in the opening stages. I'm ashamed that Peter "Strategic Mastermind" Sagan was dropped so swiftly that spectators might have thought I was riding in the opposite direction to the others.

Two groups quickly formed with a significant gap separating them, and the man at the back of the second group, stone-cold last, was me. Well. Something had to be done.

Fortunately, somebody did it. There were plenty of startled hitters in the back group, and the bizarre sight of a desperate chase in a race with 250 kilometers left lit up the streets. Not that they needed lighting up: It was one of the best atmospheres at a race that you or I are ever likely to experience. The various nations' traveling fans bellowed their support, naturalized US-based Europeans cheered on their representatives from the old countries, American cycling fans kept up a steady chant of U-S-A! and enthusiastic locals yelled with excitement at the whole spectacle.

The two groups came back together, and the rest of the first half of the marathon race was a bit calmer. The Dutch, Belgian, and German teams kept it quick enough to stay relatively tidy, but not so fast that it was uncomfortable. There's a complicated qualification process for the world's that essentially means that the bigger cycling nations get more places, so the Slovakia team of three swashbuckling pirates could just hang in and let the big guns of the heavy battleships boom out at the front. With the biggest field in cycling—nearly 200 riders—it's good to make it hard and shell out those who aren't strong enough to last the course as early as possible, and the big teams do a good job.

The first move to cause genuine concern came with a couple of laps to go, when the Great Britain team set up Ian Stannard for a bullish attack. I knew him to be a strong guy from the early northern classics where he had become a real force, and his attack led to a regrouping and a very tidy little breakaway going clear. I bit my lip, sucked my teeth, and told myself there was a long way to go, that it was no time to panic, and there were big teams that would want this escape closed down. There was no denying that a group of Michal Kwiato (the defending champion), Dani Moreno, Bauke Mollema, Tom Boonen, Andrey Amador, Elia Viviani, and Stannard could take the race away from the rest of us if things went their way.

The good thing about having fast guys like Viviani, Boonen, and Kwiato in there is you can be sure the others won't fancy dragging them to the finish line only to eat their dust. And the good thing about having fast guys like those three together is that they will be eyeing each other too closely to totally commit to the attack. Stay calm, I told myself for the 100th time, and keep riding.

It was really fast now: 225, 230, 240, 245 kilometers gone. I was feeling absolutely shafted, but I knew that if I was feeling that way, the others were probably hammered too. I was aware of the one shot that I had in the chamber, the one big payment that I could spend, and knew that I couldn't afford to blow it at the wrong moment.

The corners in that twisty crucial closing couple of kilometers had been causing problems right through the race, more for some riders than others. I knew that it was key to take them without scrubbing speed off if at all possible, and on the dead left-hander that led in to the final ascent of Libby Hill, I took a very wide line and didn't touch the brakes, finding myself gaining a few places and coming out of the bend fast. Zdeněk Štybar, a great bike handler, had a similar idea and put his head down and went for it. I tried to control my breathing and stay within myself, but truth be told, I was very close to my limit at this point, just one of the remaining hopefuls strung out behind the Czech rider.

Nobody went clear, and on the next corner, a dead right-hander at the base of the climb up 23rd Street, I tried the old trick again, taking it wide with the intention of being catapulted out of it compared to those taking the shorter inside line but needing to brake.

Greg Van Avermaet now led. I'd been pleased he hadn't been in that earlier break as I would have been really up against it then. Not only is he strong with characteristics similar to mine, he doesn't mind putting in a shift of work, and they would have been all the more dangerous with him on board. Greg hit the cobbles of 23rd Street and fired his cannonball, his one shot.

People asked me afterward if 15 laps give you the time to plan the point of your attack to precision. I have to say that it wasn't like that at all. I was trying to stay at the front and use the corners, but, for sure, there was no way I had targeted this climb as my launchpad. But with the speed I'd carried out of the corner, I hit the cobbled stretch at a big rate of knots and quickly realized that it was now or never. Two kilometers to go. I could see that if I could match Greg's effort, the speed I had from the corner would carry me by him, so I gave it everything I had and reached the top maybe five meters in front of him. I could taste metallic blood in my throat, and my calves were screaming at me with all the accumulated pain of 260 kilometers. The race was nowhere near won and my fuel gauge was glued to E. Fortunately, the next section was downhill, and I squatted flat on the crossbar in the way I had become accustomed. Maybe this was the day when people began to wonder if it was actually a useful technique rather than a trick like a wheelie or a bunny hop, as I belted down to a 90-degree left-hander and trusted my tires to hold the line, offered up a quick prayer, ignored the brakes, and leaned my Specialized over at the sort of angle the designers would cringe at. By the time I'd leveled out again, miraculously upright, Greg and

Edvald Boasson Hagen were still chasing, but were looking a bit smaller in the rearview mirror. Perfect, except there were a horribly draggy 800 meters separating me from the line and far fewer meters between me and them.

I put it in the biggest gear I dared and did my best to relax my breathing, to slow down the world around me as it passed by. The noise was at a pitch and level that was beyond anything I could remember at a bike race: It was like the Kwaremont, but with an intensity you'll only hear at the finish and when the flags of nations are inspiring extra effort from both those bursting their lungs on bikes and those bursting eardrums on the barriers. I tried to shut it out, forcing myself to use that core strength to push the pedals down in straight lines and resting my forearms on the bars to keep myself from rocking to and fro.

How badly did I want to win? That's the challenge I asked of myself. Some races you can make the finale hard by attacking and continually trying to outmuscle everyone. These are the races where people say, "Oh, well done, Sagan, or Greg, or Fabian, or Tomeke, or Kwiato, you were the strongest . . . but you didn't win." Today was not that race. This was the one-shot race, the one bullet that I had been waiting the whole year, my whole career, my whole life, to fire. I wasn't going to lose without having tried to win. I wasn't going to die wondering. But still, I was convinced I would be caught.

Looking at the video footage now, two things strike me: The first is that it doesn't look like a hill. My God, it felt like the Mur de Grammont to me. Secondly, they look miles behind. Let me tell you, I was convinced I could feel Edvald Boasson Hagen's cold Scandinavian breath on the back of my neck all the way up that final horrific 600 meters of Governor's Hill.

Needing to find some speed from somewhere, I abandoned my attempt to stay Zen and calm, and stood on the pedals and dropped it down a cog. At this point, I suffered one of the most heart-attack-inducing moments of a career littered with scary moments, when my dumb ugly riding style and twisted hip contrived to yank my foot out of the pedal. I could have easily lost all momentum, swerved across the road and been passed within sight of the line and finished 30th. I could have face-planted and become the subject of the most-watched clip on YouTube of all time. I could have slowed momentarily and lost the sprint due to the interruption in speed. Fortunately, my shoe plates stayed true, and I slotted straight back in.

In retrospect, it was the perfect nudge I needed to see me over the line. Exploding now with rage and adrenaline, I found reserves that had been hiding. *Peter, you idiot! They're coming! They're coming!*

In fact, when I finally accepted with 50 meters to go that it might well be that I was going to win, the chasers were probably no closer than when I'd looked back after the downhill plunge into that sketchy left-hander a couple of minutes earlier.

They'd closed the gap slightly by the time I rolled over the line, but by then I'd had a few seconds to sit up, shake my head in delighted wonderment, and acknowledge those people on the other side of the barriers who had done so much to make this the moment that changed my life forever.

PART TWO

Doha

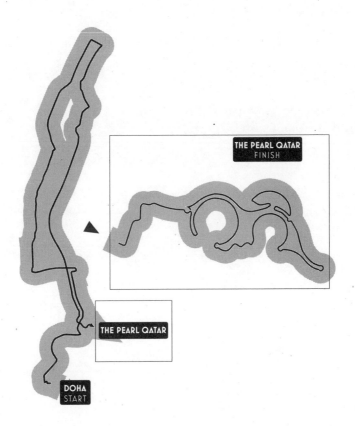

WINTER

Understanding that I was going to win in those last few yards shaped the next few minutes significantly. It's a big deal to know you are the new UCI World Champion without having to hurl your bike at the line in a desperate lunge or wait for the finish-line journalists to tell you if you got first, or wait for your soigneurs to hug you, or even wait for the official photograph to declare you victorious. To be able to grin and hold your hands aloft rather than crumpling in a heap of exhaustion is pretty special too.

I stood in the middle of the road, rolled my bike off on its own, not caring if anybody caught it (there's gratitude for you!), and lobbed my helmet into the air. Tom Boonen caught my eye as he came over the line a few moments later and, to the credit of the great man, instead of thumping his bars in frustration at an opportunity missed, he gave me a big grin and a high five, as did Elia Viviani and Zdeněk Štybar.

There was a little bit of fuss when I felt some of the congratulations were getting a bit over the top. Around the podium, press hyperbole began to spin out of control, and I turned the conversation to the refugee crisis in Europe. I don't know if you remember what it was like in the summer of 2015, but there were stories every day about desperate people dying as they tried to flee places that they once called home. I wasn't declaring myself to be a self-appointed ambassador or anything; I just felt a bit uncomfortable that folk were lining up to kiss my feet while there was more important stuff going on in the world.

But in my world? Yeah, it was a big deal . . . 2015 had been the backdrop for both the lowest moments of my career and the highest.

OK, I ought to admit at this point that I had decided that I definitely didn't want to retire anymore. It had been serious: the overtraining, the firing of Bjarne Riis, the disagreements with Bobby Julich, the total lack of form, the hip problem, the pressure from the team, the supposed contract renegotiations, the disillusion that had settled on me; all these issues had taken their toll.

But California, Patxi, Team Peter, and bike riding had brought me back. All those things, yes. But one thing in particular. Having a woman as amazing as Katarina beside me had given me reserves of strength that I didn't know I had, and I was going to make damn sure of two things: one, that she knew how much I loved her, and two, that I wasn't going to let her get away from me easily.

And so it was in Slovakia, in the bosom of our families and friends, that we were married less than two months after I'd become UCI World Champion.

There are a few things that I need to clear up about our wedding, as people seem to ask me about it all the time.

One of the reasons for such interest is that we didn't want a celebrity wedding. We had lots of people trying to get access, pay us money, or even just get an invitation, but as far as we were concerned, that was not in the spirit of such an occasion. So if you can't find much on YouTube, it's because of that. Our wedding day was a mixture of Slovak traditions, more traditions from Katarina's hometown of Dolný Kubín, and some fun stuff that we dreamt up between us.

We got married in Dolný Kubín. In preparation, I bought a white Cadillac to deliver us to the service, but the thing rather inauspiciously broke down the day before. Not to be thwarted in my desire to arrive at my wedding in a really special car, I went out and got my hands on the next best thing: an old green Trabant.

My friend Martin was driving, and we coughed and spluttered through all of the friends and locals who had turned out to wish us well. The first stop we had to make was not at the church, but outside Katarina's family home to complete an important tradition. To be honest, I'm not sure if this is a Slovakian ritual or maybe just something they do in Dolný Kubín, as I've never seen it before. But I was confronted by a slender tree trunk laid across her driveway and presented with a rusty old hacksaw. It is the groom's job to cut clean through the wood before he can proceed, so I set to it. After a few minutes of me huffing and puffing with the blunted blade, the crowd was beginning to get restless. As I started to build up a bit of heat and get a bead of sweat on under the heavy Slovakian wedding suit I was wearing, I began to wonder if we should have arrived the day before to get started, but then, thankfully, the cavalry arrived. Or rather Martin, appearing at my shoulder with a gas-powered chainsaw that a sympathetic local had rustled up. Much more my style, and the gold brocade that adorned my traditional outfit was now more at risk from sawdust than perspiration.

Vroom. Crunch. Thank God for that chainsaw. I might still be there now, ploughing my lonely little groove in the wood with that ancient blade while Katarina frowned at her watch on the church steps and her hair turned as white as her dress. I love a tradition as much as the next man, but I was planning on getting married that day.

Job done, and we were back in the Trabant like Batman and Robin and racing off down the street at a speed very nearly quicker than walking pace, the engine roaring at a pitch nowhere near as impressive as the chainsaw.

Religion and the whole way of life within the Catholic church is a rock to most of us Slovakians. Seeing the beautiful woman whom I was going to spend the rest of my life with in her wedding dress walk up the historic steps of Saint Catherine's was an emotional moment for me, to the extent that I can barely bring to mind the service that followed. All I can picture when I try to think about it now is Katarina, radiant in that incredible white dress and veil.

A little way out of Dolný Kubín, a sheer cliff face of limestone hulks above a bend in the River Orava. The narrow platform of rock that sits on top of the impressive formation has been home for at least a thousand years to the incredible Castle Orava. This is where the notoriously spooky silent film *Nosferatu* was shot in the 1920s, and we picked it as a dramatic backdrop for our celebrations.

We'd spent many an enjoyable evening chatting over dinner about doing something that people would remember. You only get married once, so it seemed to us that pictures of us standing on a lawn, or in front of a hotel, would be . . . well, they'd be nice, but we could dress up and go into the garden any time. This was going to be a one-off, and we wanted the pictures to be unique too. We had Nosferatu's castle: What next? In the end, we called in our photographer friend Jakub Klimo to design something, and he came up with another stunt that people often ask me about. I had to wriggle out of that suit, get rigged up with a stunt-man's harness, then put the suit back on over the top. Then, I was hoisted into the air and lowered onto a narrow bar about 6 meters above the ground. Awaiting me there was a sort of tiny Victorian trick bike that looked as if it had been whisked through time from a nineteenth century sideshow carnival. Below me, continuing the sort of H. G. Wells steampunk theme, people gathered in Dickensian hats and bonnets, just as huge clouds of smoke began to billow around them. Through their midst, resplendent in her stunning wedding dress, strode Katarina, pulling at strings that appeared to operate me and my stunt bike in the sky like an inverse puppet show. To be honest, I have no real explanation for this one, you'll have to ask Jakub, but it was certainly a lot of fun.

Mr. and Mrs. Sagan. It felt good.

———

Giovanni was ahead of the game that winter. I thought I was pretty much on top of my life, managing to meet the commercial responsibilities that the team expected of me and the growing list of personal endorsements and arrangements that we'd picked up, as well as finding time for friends, family, and kicking back, but still training hard enough to win more races and honor the UCI rainbow jersey.

I was wrong.

It was like a switch clicked on somewhere in the ether the second I crossed that finish line in Richmond, and a whole globe full of people who had been blissfully unaware of my existence until that moment suddenly wanted—no, needed—to talk to me. The attention you receive for being an athlete at a certain level has always been a curious but not unpleasant side effect of success for me. I've always enjoyed it up to a point; that point is when I close my front door and shut the world out, or climb onto the team bus with my teammates, or, best of all, when I'm on my bike in the company of the professional peloton. Now, there was no letup.

In those months after Richmond, my time wasn't my own, and it was difficult to make out the light at the end of the tunnel. How can I describe it? Imagine you're swimming in a warm, blue sea, with clear water below you and the sun tickling your shoulders. Nice, eh? Now imagine that you can't see land any more. Not so good. Actually, the experience hasn't changed, but the fear that you may go under before it relents has shifted the perspective drastically.

I began to have an insight into the so-called curse of the rainbow jersey, where former world champions had followed up the best day of their lives with a harrowing season of poor results. Curses were nothing to do with it: The slump in form was surely much more likely to have been caused by the interruption to their carefully crafted training programs and lives beyond the bike.

This is where having an agent who is a shrewd businessman, a trusted friend, and also a former top rider is a crucial advantage. Instead of instantly cashing in on the opportunities beating a path to the Team Peter front door, Giovanni knew that this was precisely the moment where we had to take most care of my career.

He and I talked at length about what we should do to help me stay focused. Focused and happy: We both knew I win nothing when I'm miserable.

This is the point where I shine a little more light on the second-most important adult in my life, my constant companion, my sidekick, the incomparable and long-suffering Gabriele Uboldi.

Gabriele was already in the Tinkoff setup, looking after all of us riders as a press officer. In a big cycling team, you tend to get quite close to your PR guys, more so than in other sports, because the nature of being on the road and so close to the public means they are key components in keeping the team functioning. After all, the whole point of funding a professional cycling team is to generate publicity, so you can't just pull the blinds down. You have to find a balance between giving something of yourself to the followers of the sport, preparing and racing to the best of your abilities, and keeping a sliver of yourself for those closest to you. People like Gabriele become part of the squad, just like riders, directors, coaches, soigneurs, and mechanics.

Foreseeing the issues that the extra attention of being world champion would bring, Giovanni approached Stefano Feltrin at Tinkoff to propose moving Gabriele into a role where he would be looking after me more but would still be able to keep up with his team duties and could do both jobs for the same money. We'd already approached Gabri to see if he'd be up for the switch, and he'd given us the nod after some consideration. He obviously hadn't given it enough thought, but that's Gabri.

However, things didn't go to plan. Feltrin believed there was no way Gabriele could be spared from his team duties and that we'd all just have to dig in, work hard, and embrace the extra attention coming my way.

Now, something you may not know about me, and I don't think it's come up before now, is that I love a fire extinguisher. Some people are crazy about setting things on fire. I'm mad about putting them out. Come on, who among us can put hand on heart and say they have never ever thought: *Ooh, look at that. Shiny and red. Fun, surely?*

Take that house that I had built in Žilina, for example. The one with the garage, the bedroom, the gym, and not much else that ended up becoming the Centro Sportive. Well, when it was finished, I had some friends over to celebrate, as you do, and of course, there had to be a fire-extinguisher moment. It took a gang of professional cleaners three visits to get rid of it all. The white stuff floats in the air, waiting for the cleaners to do their job and leave, then gently sinks down to the floor, and leaves a new fine layer over everything.

Not everybody shares my enthusiasm for the fire extinguisher, so I spend most days reining in my natural urges to snuff out nonexistent conflagrations, but every now and then, it feels like the right thing to do.

Like, for instance, when the Tinkoff team was in Poreč on the Istrian coast for a winter training camp, the day after Stefano Feltrin had turned down Giovanni's request to move Gabriele to become my full-time manager, assistant, and minder. There, in the crowded hotel lobby, with teammates, staff, hotel staff, and other guests milling around, it was clear to me that everybody would get a real lift if I were to drench them all with a fire extinguisher.

The next morning, Feltrin was on the phone to Gabriele, telling him that he'd had an idea: How would he like to become Peter Sagan's full-time assistant? At least I think he said "assistant." It might have been "fire-extinguisher banisher."

From that point on, where I go, Gabri goes. It's been a huge change for me and positive in every way. Now I can concentrate on riding, racing, relaxing, and spending maximum time with my family instead of rushing around and worrying if I've forgotten something: passport, kit, senses. He does all the worrying, fields as much as possible himself, and gets me to where I need to be. Now, if Gabri says I need to do something, I know that thing has already been tested and prodded to see if it really needs me to do it, so I accept it without question.

It doesn't feel like he keeps me out of trouble, but I suppose he does in that we fill the time with other stuff. As well as the constant bets, dares, and challenges, all that dead time between training, racing, and commercial stuff is now filled with PS4 rather than fire extinguishers. There are long hours in hotels when there's not enough time to go home, but still time to fill. That's when Gabri comes into his own. He is the perfect FIFA 18 opponent: willing, enthusiastic, not useless, but not as good as me. He will tell you that he lets me win because it's good for my morale before races. If that were true, then he'd still win the odd game now and then, just to keep it realistic. This is sadly beyond him. I am Barcelona, and he is Juventus, which is a great window on our characters: I get a wild joy out of simply playing the game, he takes pleasure in trying to stop others enjoying themselves. And fails.

On Tinkov

Cycling has always been the most commercial of commercial sports—what other sport can you think of where the name of the team is the name of their sponsor? Cristiano Ronaldo plays for Juventus, but if he was a cyclist, he'd ride for Samsung. The people with the money play more obvious and less altruistic roles than in other professional sports. In cycling, we are told about the appeal of sponsor airtime and exposure for their brand.

Bike companies like Scott or Trek continue as headline sponsors because the link to their customers is easy to understand, and pro riders emblazoned with their names and logos, using their gear are the best possible showcase for their excellence.

Apart from that, pretty much every top cycling team is sponsored by a company run by individuals who are passionate about the sport and want to be involved. Even Sky, a team held up as being the logical conclusion for all things commercial, is reportedly run as the personal project of cycling-mad James Murdoch. He is in good company, as most teams have a driving influence pushing them along, somebody who does it because they can afford it and they love it.

There is no finer example than Oleg Tinkov.

As it happens, he is a friend of Chelsea's Roman Abramovich, the man he most resembles from other sports. Both fiercely competitive businessmen who, after the collapse of the Soviet Union, saw their chances to build empires of their own, they get a tremendous kick out of assembling the team of their own choice then cheering it to victory. Who wouldn't?

As characters though, they are very different. I don't know Abramovich, but he seems like a very quiet guy, completely impervious to requests for interviews, keeping his opinions to himself and happy to bask in the reflective glory of his club's successes.

That doesn't sound much like Oleg.

There isn't a subject that Oleg doesn't have an opinion on. And if you're talking to him about something he wasn't aware of beforehand, he'll have formed a view on it before you've finished asking the question.

His brain is incredible, constantly analyzing, constantly asking, "What if?" and floating a new idea every waking minute.

Every one of these ideas is vocalized, whether it's smart, out-landish, or flat-out crazy. He doesn't have that filter that most people have, the one that runs something through internally for us before delivering it to the outside world. As you can imagine, his capacity to offend is limitless, but he is also fantastic, engaging, and provocative company.

With Oleg, there is always something going on. His energy is unbelievable. He wants to ride with us all the time, then we'd all go to the best restaurants, drink the best wine, stay in the best hotels. He is a great example of somebody who is really trying to live life every day.

Of course, on the flipside, differences of opinion with Oleg are inevitable. His whole ethos is to challenge and to find different ways of doing things, but it is hard to fall out with him too. He never once "played" me. If he wanted to tell you some bad news, he wouldn't dress it up, get somebody else to do it, or sweep it under the carpet. He'd just tell you. You were shit today, Peter. But you tried, so fuck it, let's go eat. Do you fancy caviar?

We worked hard every day, but we had fun every day. It was the giddiest fairground ride at the carnival, and I didn't hear too many people complaining about it. He could argue with you, lose his temper with you, and threaten you, but five minutes later, he'd be topping your glass up and telling you some joke or funny anecdote from the day.

He was good to us, recognizing the value of Team Peter, and agreeing to take us all on board as a package despite the expense and the disruption to the other people already working on the team. He constantly wanted more from everyone, but you could see that it came from his own drive and restless spirit, not entitlement or disappointment.

And when he got fed up with owning a cycling team, he dumped it. Just like that.

Will he be back? I wouldn't bet against it. Ask him about the Tour de France and a gleam comes into his eye straightaway. Without a win in the Tour, despite his best efforts, he clearly sees it as unfinished business.

I'd be the first to welcome him back. He's straight talking, totally transparent, and unwaveringly straight. Sure, he's hard to work for, but everybody is hard to work for in their own way. The best jobs are rarely the easiest jobs. Would I work for him again? I hope I never have to answer that question for real because in some ways I feel like I've done my Oleg time, and I've earned a quieter life. But he has a way of making you feel like you need to be part of what he's trying to do and that he can't possibly do it without you.

My own answer is to commit myself to BORA-hansgrohe for the rest of my career. It's perfect for me, and then I don't have to even think about working for anybody else again ever.

To that end, Giovanni has just agreed to another three years with them, which is a very long time in cycling, and I hope it doesn't end there. I don't want to move away from somewhere that gives me so much trust, love, support, and belief.

But Oleg Tinkov sure was a lot of fun to be around.

SPRING

"Christmas Day in Belgium."

That's how Fabian Cancellara described the Tour of Flanders, De Ronde van Vlaanderen, or if you're Flemish, just De Ronde. I know exactly what he meant. A fixed day on the calendar, the first Sunday in April, which divides the year into things that happen before De Ronde and things that happen after it. To indulge Fabian's analogy a bit longer, there is an equally eagerly anticipated race a week later, the heavily fêted Paris–Roubaix, standing in for New Year. Some people like Christmas, others prefer New Year, but most of us get a kick out of both, and they each loom large in our headlights as we approach and then recede wistfully in our rearview mirrors when they're gone.

Most teams seriously targeting the northern classics will make the region their home for a couple of weeks. In the old days,

Gent–Wevelgem (Roubaix's little brother) used to take place on the Wednesday between them, but since I've been a professional rider, Gent–Wevelgem takes place the weekend before, heaping even more prestige on what is known as "Cobbles Fortnight," especially if you're Flemish. The space between the big races has helped to nurture the popularity of the supporting events too, with midweek rendezvous like E3 Harelbeke or Dwars Door Vlaanderen now looking like hefty cornerstones on any cyclists' *palmarès*.

The most notable spring of my early career was 2013, when I won my first classic. I became Gent–Wevelgem champion by jumping away from the lead group with 4 kilometers remaining as everybody was eyeing up a sprint. What I remember most about that day was how unbelievably cold it was, with enough snow around that the organizers were forced to lop 50-odd kilometers off the distance.

De Ronde that year was my third classic. I came into it on the crest of that Gent–Wevelgem win and a second place in Milan–San Remo. When I found myself shoulder to shoulder with Fabian Cancellara on the race's last obstacle, the Paterberg, I began to think that maybe my time had arrived.

The Paterberg is just 400 meters long. Despite the cobbles and the gradient, anybody can ride up it. But coming as it does less than 15 kilometers from the finish line, it can be a springboard for success or a graveyard of ambitions. In 2013, it was the latter for me: 240 kilometers of racing had left indelible dents in my legs, and Fabian, by then a Monument winner four times over, dealt me a coup de grâce on the steepest stretch of pavé. A few short bike lengths out of reach at the top was a whopping 90 seconds by the time I reached the line in Oudenaarde. Second place at Flanders was a good result, but I was going to need to improve in the finale of the longest, hardest races if I was ever going to be a match for the likes of Fabian.

————

Forward to 2016. What had changed for me during the three years since that lesson on the Paterberg? Well, on the plus side, I had won one of the events synonymous with endurance and the world's. Richmond was a 261-kilometer race, and I had delivered the goods on the hardest stretch of the last lap. But in the debit column, there was a still a yawning gap next to the Monuments. Those second places back in 2013 had been as close as I'd come to a title. OK, I'd won a couple of big one-day races that might like to call themselves classics—Gent–Wevelgem and E3 Harelbeke—but I was acutely aware that though they might be tough races with high-quality fields, both of them had been massively shorter than the Monument I craved. It was something that I needed to address.

Milan–San Remo had looked good for me. I'd got over all the capi without any undue fuss and cleared the Poggio with the leaders. Into the final few hundred meters and with the remaining contenders stretched out enticingly, I was sitting about five wheels from the front, where Edvald Boasson Hagen was looking over his shoulder and trying to decide whether he should go for broke or if somebody else would take on the sprint first. As we slowed momentarily, Fernando Gaviria got himself on the wrong side of the wheel in front; Greg Van Armamaet's, I think. He slammed into the ground on his left hip, right under my front wheel. It was one of those crashes you can see coming, where it feels like you're watching an action replay while it's unfolding in front of you, so I was able to brake and dodge him to the left. Unsurprisingly, this didn't do an awful lot for my sprint. All momentum gone, the line I'd been following scrubbed out, the gap to those behind instantly closed . . . I had a go, but it was a lost cause, and I was well back on the winner, Arnaud Démare.

So that was another long race that I had been in contention for at the death, which was good, but it was hard to read too much into it. Milan–San Remo is a beautiful race, but you don't take the same hard kicking you do at Flanders or Roubaix, and I hadn't really had the chance to test my sprint at the end of 250 kilometers.

Next stop was Gent–Wevelgem. This race is shaped by the weather more than any other. The long, flat exposed parts of the course are often battered by winds howling off the English

Channel, and when that westerly blows, it usually carries the promise of rain or sometimes snow. The 2016 race began splitting as soon as we left the start in Deinze. I'm sure someone can tell you why it starts in Deinze and not in Gent. The same guy would probably advise you not to try walking to the start of Paris–Roubaix from Paris and may be able to explain why the Tour de France only starts in France every other year.

After a couple of hours of trying to keep your nose out of the wind while staying near enough to the front that you don't get caught on the wrong side of any splits, the race enters its tricky section. While not as nasty as De Ronde, there is no hiding place in Gent–Wevelgem, and some of the hills are longer and higher than those waiting for the peloton a week later.

The key climb is the Kemmelberg, a ridge of such obvious strategic advantage in World War I that many, many young men lost their lives on its slopes in a tragic series of battles. In fact, those sorry dark days a century ago are rarely far from the action at Gent–Wevelgem: The race skirts countless immaculate cemeteries of all sizes and even passes under the Menin Gate, the unforgettable memorial to all those who were lost but whose final resting place remains unknown.

The Kemmelberg is probably the best known and hardest climb in Flanders not to feature in De Ronde, situated far to the west from the crouching bergs that characterize it. For the first time in any of the current pelotons' lifetimes, we tackled this hill from the steeper "other" side; where the cobbles rise up to a fearsome 23 percent. It features twice: early on when the field is harrowed, then at a decisive point before the run back to the finish. I was feeling good when we hit the Kemmelberg for the second time and went hard, straight up the middle. The cobbles are neat, and the road is broad, unlike, say, the Koppenberg, and there is less danger of getting caught up in traffic if you're not right at the head of affairs. Over the top, it was me, Cancellara (of course), Sep Vanmarcke, and Viacheslav Kuznetsov. We only had a few seconds, but with all four of us pulling, we held off the others for the remaining 34 kilometers to reach Wevelgem.

We didn't slow until the last few hundred meters, when Fabian found himself on the front. Both he and I tried exploratory moves to try to get the others to play their cards early, but nobody was fooled. The denouement began strangely, as Kuznetsov and Fabian began sprinting at the same moment on opposite sides of the wide road. I chose the Katusha rider's wheel, but his jump was a powerful one, and it took a massive effort to get into his slipstream. All four of us came back together in the center of the road with less than 200 meters to go, and I had to go again, to get around Kuznetsov. Crossing the line, it looked more comfortable than it had been. My second Gent–Wevelgem.

It had been 240 kilometers with a hard sprint at the death. But it wasn't a Monument. Was I where I needed to be? We'd find out in seven days.

———

So. Christmas Day in Belgium, though it was more than that for Fabian Cancellara: It was his final Tour of Flanders. He was retiring after the most glittering career in the sport's recent history. A time trial specialist from one of cycling's less storied nations, "Spartacus" flat out refused to be pigeonholed and became one of the best classics riders of this, or any, generation. He had ridden back-to-back Flanders and Roubaix victories twice! Nothing would make him happier than to finish with an eighth—yes, eighth—Monument victory.

It was unseasonably warm in Belgium that weekend. Brought out by the April sunshine, the crowds were vast, half a dozen deep on the Oude Kwaremont, with not a corner of temporary decking or corporate marquee left to stand on or under. De Ronde goes up this climb three times now, making it a key strategic point in the race. The main part of the climb is narrow and cobbled, but not super steep, so it's not the ideal springboard for a race-winning attack. What does make it tricky is the extra couple of kilometers of cobbled false flat that carries on after the nominal summit has been topped, so while it might not be the place to win the race, losing it here is easily done.

The first two ascents of the Kwaremont had played their part in whittling things down, and with 30-odd kilometers left to race, the favorites were in a group of 20 or so riders closing in on a break that had been away most of the day.

The first time I raced against Michal Kwiato, we were both about 14. Being the same age and riding out of the junior programs in Slovakia and Poland respectively when we were kids means that we know each other well. Our styles have often been compared, and I guess from the outside, we do have similar attributes, mostly relating to our ability to contend in varying types of races and conditions. Maybe it was that familiarity that set my senses tingling when Kwiato clipped off the front of that group of favorites. We were on an apparently innocuous stretch of paved road as it wiggled through some straggly houses somewhere round the back of Ronse, with all the team leaders marshalling any remaining teammates in preparation for the last climbs of the race. I pushed on the pedals a little harder and rode up to his wheel as he accelerated away from the remnants of the bunch and tucked into his slipstream.

Unsurprisingly, he was keen for me to come through and give him a turn, but I wasn't sure there was going to be anything in it for me. There are always plenty of tentative or abortive moves in these nervous late stages of big races, and I didn't want to waste an effort unnecessarily. However, when Sep Vanmarcke put in a big effort to bridge across to us a few moments later, the three of us looked at each other and agreed with a quick nod: We ride.

Over the undulating roads that remained between us and the bottom of the final ascent of the Oude Kwaremont, we pushed hard, each of us spending no more than a few seconds on the front on any turn. The shared effort was enough to hold off an increasingly concerned main race group. As we passed the last of the houses in Kluisbergen—there are always two old ladies here, in folding chairs listening to a transistor radio at ear-splitting volume, you can't miss them—we had a handful of seconds over our competitors. I led on to the Kwaremont and charged up the crest of the pavé, trying to tread that tightrope between riding as hard as I could without entirely emptying the tank.

There were actually eight of us at the front of the race, which at this point had only 18 kilometers remaining. In effect, though, Kwiato and Vanmarcke were the only two with me, as the other five were survivors of the day-long break that we had just caught and were hanging on gamely for high finishing positions.

It can be difficult for fans at the side of the road to appreciate a race situation. Cyclists move fast, the peloton can be a swarm of changing colors and personalities with individuals hard to pick out. The popularity of certain helmets and sunglasses have made quick recognition of the riders involved in the action even more difficult. It was this that led to the early innovation of colored jerseys for the leaders of Grand Tours and, in turn, the honor of wearing the rainbow jersey as reigning world champion. As my three seasons of holding that jersey have unfolded, I've begun to understand and feel the expectation that comes with wearing a badge that lets people know who you are. But I think, looking back, that it was on this final ascent of the Kwaremont in 2016 when I first realized what the rainbow jersey can do. The noise was just immense, a roaring corridor of sustained sound. At the time I was just concentrating on driving as hard as I could to hold off the chasers, but looking at it on the video now, I can see it from the spectators' point of view: the rainbow jersey charging up one of the most atmospheric climbs in the sport trying to win their treasured race. The identity of the wearer was secondary. For them, it was the world champion bouncing off the cobbles below them, not Peter Sagan or another Tinkoff, Quick-Step, or Trek rider. Halfway up the Kwaremont, something unexpected happened. Kwiato, who had been so forceful and sharp in creating this opportunity, began to falter. I sensed that he was going through the pain that I had suffered here three years previously— 240 kilometers? No problem. But 255 might as well be 355 when that moment strikes.

As Vanmarcke and I rode through the square at the top of the climb and onto the false flat, an even bigger roar chased us on from behind. Fabian Cancellara had ridden up the Oude Kwaremont for the final time in his career, and surely this was the quickest of all his ascents of the famous old stretch of cobbles. He had passed Kwiato and everybody else who had been with us at the bottom of the short climb, and now he was breathing down our necks.

Off the pounding of the cobbles at last, Vanmarcke gave me a turn on the main road. He was born a short ride from here, a Flandrian through and through, and I know how much strength that can give a rival. We were now at that strange sporting conundrum that only cycling delivers: Each of you is forced to rely on the other to give you both the best chance of winning, while simultaneously being acutely aware that you are also each other's biggest rival for that same victory.

The Paterberg is a funny little road. No matter how many times you ride it, it still comes as a surprise when you turn right onto it because there really shouldn't be a road there. In fact, there hadn't always been a road there. The story is that the guy who owned the field that the Paterberg climbs over was such a cycling fan that he actually built the road to attract the race to come past his front door. Whatever the truth of the tale, it is a nasty little berg with a horribly steep passage at the top.

When Vanmarcke and I hit the pavé, there was no time for hanging around or tactics. Cancellara had won this race three times, and he had us in his crosshairs. The last climb of the Tour of Flanders, the last cobbles of De Ronde, just a couple of hundred meters of pain, then only 13 kilometers to the line.

As we approached the steepest part of the climb, shoulder to shoulder, I could picture myself in this very same spot 36 months ago, in a two-man break with a slender advantage at the end of a crushingly hard race. On that occasion, I had been asked searching questions, and I'd come up short of answers. Had I changed?

As the cobbles reared up to 20 percent, I locked the upper part of my body, sat solid in the saddle, and tried to imagine my legs as pistons driving the engine. Beside me, Vanmarcke stood on his pedals and tried to dance over the pavé. Beside me, then no longer beside me. He dropped away in those last few yards, and I swung round the 90-degree bend at the summit on my own. Cancellara came around the corner just 15 seconds behind me, the same gap I'd had on him at the bottom, but he had caught Vanmarcke in that time.

Do you remember me telling you about those last few hundred meters in Richmond when I was convinced that I would be caught? *They're coming, they're coming,* was all I could think as I gasped toward the line then. Well, this was nothing like that. If I'd had a jinx at Flanders, it was reinforced by the memory of being handed a hiding by Fabian at the top of the Paterberg. I had broken the jinx by passing that bad luck to somebody else. Two hundred and fifty-five kilometers? No problem. Show me the way.

I relaxed as much as I could. Despite being on the rivet for 150 kilometers, I felt OK. The gap went out to over 20 seconds and stayed there. Everything was going to be OK.

With 3 kilometers to go, ahead of me on the cycle path off to the left, a guy in full Molteni team kit from about 1970 was rolling along like a vision of Eddy Merckx. It's probably the most Belgian thing I've ever seen. "Eddy!" I shouted. He looked round, but it wasn't him.

A few minutes later and I was a Monument winner. I pulled a one-handed wheelie for the cameras at the finish line. It felt good.

On Sprinting

If there is one question I've been asked most often in my career, it's probably: Are you a sprinter? Or maybe it's: Why are you such a nutcase? But no, probably still: Are you a sprinter?

The answer is no. I am an all-rounder. I can sprint as well or as badly as I can climb or time trial; it's just that sprinting comes a bit easier to me.

I've still got the jump I had when I first turned pro. When we do the various tests and studies that we have to do for the team, for the UCI, for the anti-doping guys, on a good day my watts-per-kilo ratio is still as good as it's ever been, so I can still pump out a bit of power. However, I turned pro very young. I'm still only 28, so it could go at any moment. Cycling history is littered with sprinters who had one or two stellar seasons before they seemed to lose their edge. These days, it's less common. Guys

like Andre Greipel and Mark Cavendish have been among the
fastest year in, year out for many seasons. They say that Mario
Cipollini was like that too: good every year, despite the passing of time. You can't be quick for a year or two and retire with
57—57!—Grand Tour stage wins to your name, as Cipollini did.
Maybe the decrease in doping has changed things? It could well
be that. There aren't as many mystifying performances as there
used to be.

The thing to remember is that every sprint is different: One
hundred riders with one hundred different stories is one thing,
but the variables in the sprint are huge. Most big bunch sprints
come in Grand Tours, so by their very nature, they vary, as they
have a different route every year, every day. Even if a stage finishes in a town the race has visited before, there is no guarantee the line will be in the same place, or the route will cover the
same corners or rises and falls. There's also the unpredictable
element of the weather: Rain is the most obvious hazard with
corners offering the terrifying jolt of sketchy terrain and a slip-
ping tire, but every sprint is also affected by wind strength and
direction, something you might not be able to appreciate from
the view on TV.

Crashes, or just fear of crashes, play a huge part in sprinting,
of course, and you have to live by your wits a little bit. Being nervous about crashing often becomes a self-fulfilling prophecy, so

it is key to stay relaxed. After all, you don't need to be sprinting to fall off. Chris Froome once crashed into a race organizer seconds into a time trial, and we've all had an embarrassing tumble trying to clip out of the pedals at one time or another. It'll just hurt more and look more spectacular if you do it 100 meters from the finish line at the Tour de France.

I don't like sprinting from a lead-out train. It stresses me out, which is the last thing I need. Everybody is relying on you, and you have to fight for your position on the wheel in front miles before the finish. I don't like fighting in the bunch. Life is too short. That's just wasted energy when you're going to need all of it later. I prefer to just ride and keep my eyes on what's happening. That's what I'll have been doing all day anyway; it's just getting a bit quicker by this stage. If you want to win a Monument like Flanders or Roubaix, for example, the last 100 kilometers will be like the last 10 kilometers of a Grand Tour stage for me: Ride carefully, ride positively, keep your eyes open.

It's a percentages game too. If I'm left to do my own thing, without anything going drastically wrong like a crash or a course diversion, I usually finish in the top five of a sprint, without needing to weigh up the individuals I'm sprinting against. I don't want to sound immodest, but if I imagined I was somebody else watching the race, it's realistic to expect the UCI World Champion, who is known to be able to sprint pretty well, to be up there at the finish if he's in the lead group. That's just normal. With a lead-out train, you take much of your own fate out of your own hands. Sure, it's nice for someone like Mark Cavendish when that Omega Pharma–Quick-Step train he used to have with Tony Martin, Mark Renshaw, and everybody drops him off with 200 meters to go, but there are so many things that can go wrong. You lose the wheel. Another team has a faster train, and your guys get burned off early. Your last guy misjudges the distance. The likely result is yes, in theory, you may have a better chance of winning, but you also have a greater chance of going nowhere. I prefer to do my own thing, and if somebody is faster than me, then he is faster than me. No problem. But I won't be far behind him. And I like podiums, even when I'm not on the top step. I'd still rather be there than in the bus, arguing with the team about what went wrong.

I suppose, in an ideal world, rather than a lead-out, I'll have a teammate nearby, just in case I can't handle things on my own. Especially in the national team, that has worked really well, with either my brother Juraj or Michal Kolář close at hand in difficult moments. One man—one good man—can get on the front and drive a group along to dissuade attacks, can drag an escapee back or give up a wheel or even his bike if I am struck by some act of God at the sharp end of a race.

One of my mantras is that it's good to have a plan, but plans don't always work. There is an old story from the salesman's manual: You're a traveling salesman, and you walk in to see a customer who has bought the same thing off you many times in the past, and he says he doesn't want any today. What do you do? You sell him something else. And that's what I have to do, too. Sell my rivals something else.

Basically, I will try to ride as "normally" as possible until the last couple of kilometers. The most common shape for stages in Grand Tours now is that the first hour of the day is a crazy rush to get somebody in a break; then it calms down. With the better communication between the team cars, riders, and race organization, people have become very experienced at knowing what is needed to bring that long escape back. And you don't want it caught too soon, as that would just encourage some other guys to go, and it gets messy again. You may feel it's unlucky when a break gets recaptured within 2 kilometers of the line after 100 kilometers out in the wind, but it's not really luck; it's the masterplan working.

So, we're all together with about 2,000 meters to go. Yes, somebody may breakaway, and you have to be alert to who it is, but if the bunch is traveling fast enough and there are sprinters' teams and lead-out trains with a lot to lose, it is unlikely to succeed. Stay cool and play close attention. With 500 meters left,

I will pick the wheel of the rider who I think is most likely to give me the best route to the line.

This is another moment where being a solo artiste is a big advantage. Let's say that at the team meeting this morning, you agreed on the order of the lead-out, who was going to pull over when, and when you would be let loose at the line. Let's say you've looked at the course in the roadbook that the race organizers give us all, and we settle on 300 meters as the ideal point to begin the sprint.

OK. Now I'm there, with 500 meters to go, the crowd is screaming, banging on the barriers with anything they can find, and the wind is in my ears as I hit 50 kilometers per hour. Suddenly, I realize there's a headwind that we hadn't planned for. No way do I want to hit the front at 300 meters, I'll just get buffeted and then swamped. How can I get that message to everybody in front of me, a-reeling and a-rocking as we already are, holding each others' wheels in the mayhem and the maelstrom of noise? No chance. That is one plan that can't be changed.

My agent, Giovanni Lombardi, was one of the lead-out men for Mario Cipollini when the Lion King was in the rainbow jersey of world champion. He told me a story that in one of Super Mario's earlier teams, they had both Cipo and Johan Museeuw, who was also really fast in those days. They claimed to have a system of whistles they could use to communicate. I find that hard to believe. There's no way you could hear, no way to change plans. It might have worked if they had some sheep to round up, perhaps.

To be honest, when it's a messy sprint with the different trains getting in each other's way, breakaways being caught, lead-out men pulling over, that's when it suits me best. Without anybody else to worry about, it's easy for me to change plans.

Take Australia in 2018, for instance. It was my first race of the year, literally the first time the rainbow jersey had been seen since the podium in Norway. I had no condition and no real expectation. I was there to get fitter in the warm weather, to chill out away from the media frenzy in Europe, and to enjoy a bit of bike racing. The real training would begin in the Sierra Nevada in Spain, a month later. In that Australian race, if I'd had a train, I would have said, "Forget it, guys, not today; we're not here to win this one." Or if I'd not felt too bad and felt I owed the team a result, we could have organized, and I would have stressed about staying with them and not letting them bury themselves for me without good reason. With half a dozen hammers battering away for your benefit, you want to make sure that if you're the nail, you'd better be sharp.

None of that, thank goodness. I just enjoyed the ride in warm weather, wearing shorts and short sleeves. All of a sudden, there were 2 kilometers left. I got focused, and the rainbow jersey had its first win of the year. Nice.

There are some basic rules to follow. If it's a downhill finish, or fast because of a tailwind, I like to start farther back from the front than usual, so you can hit top speed before you get to the front. That creates a bit more momentum and makes you harder to catch. If there's a headwind, then you want to stay covered up until the last possible moment. Preferably, get on the wheel of the sprinter with the most powerful train, as they are likely to drop him off earlier than he would like, and you can use his speed for an ultra-late charge as he begins to die away in the wind.

Uphill sprints need fewer tactics. It's usually just a macho strength battle, and the strongest guy of the day will be the winner, which isn't always the case in other finishes. If it gets too steep, I am likely to get out-punched by the real climbers . . . I'm thinking about Purito Rodriguez and Chris Froome when the Tour de France finished on the Mur de Huy, for example.

Apart from that, I love those messy sprints when everybody is all over the road, and I can duck and dive my way to the line. I've never ridden the Giro d'Italia, and maybe I will one day, but I have a feeling I'd like the finishes there. They always seem to have a 90-degree bend 50 meters from the line or something crazy like that, finishes so narrow you could reach out and touch both barriers. Plus, they tend to go through the finish line and then do a lap of the town before the end of the stage, so you can have a good look at it in advance. One day, maybe.

So, that's all there is to it. You have all my secrets. Not really secrets, just common sense, but it's all I've got to give you. It's up to you now!

SUMMER

The Olympics are amazing, aren't they? What else, across the whole of life, culture, and the entire human experience, can bring together so many people from across the globe? I remember racing home from school to see Slovakian athletes going up against the world's best at the games in Atlanta or Sydney, and the snowy, dark nights screaming at the TV as our ice hockey heroes competed in the Winter Olympics.

Olympic road cycling is odd, though. To begin with, the peculiarly unique situation in cycling where a team sport gives up an individual winner is a difficult concept that sits uncomfortably alongside the other feats of personal achievement on show. Track cycling works well, but the format of road cycling is a lot less applicable to the Olympic setup than many of the other sports represented.

There's also the matter of cycling's late arrival at the party. Atlanta in 1996 was the first time that professional cyclists were invited to compete in the Olympics, meaning that the Olympic champion has been viewed as a respected curiosity rather than the solid plank of cycling history that attends the world championships, which hardly seems fair. You don't even get a jersey. I know the first Olympic champion of the modern era, Pascal Richard, ran into trouble with the IOC when he tried to have the Olympic rings incorporated into his team kit. Sammy Sánchez, the winner in Beijing, came up with the idea of adding a bit of gold to his kit, a compromise that has stuck and keeps the IOC off the champion's back.

I went to London in 2012, optimistic that I could produce something in the road race. Team Great Britain team had spent the preceding months telling the world how they were going to control the race, to give Mark Cavendish the best chance of adding an Olympic title to his world's victory. Ján Valach, the DS of the Slovakian squad, thought that they would find this very difficult in the latter stages with the small team sizes and the unchallenging circuit, but they were very welcome to try, and I agreed with him. As did all the other teams as it turned out. I basically dozed my way round the English countryside for a few hours, 10 times up the same shallow hill, thinking that if I kept Cav in sight I'd be OK. In the run-in back to London, the

GB team, tired from a long summer's day on the sharp end of the bunch, understandably began to wilt, the race fractured, and Alexander Vinokourov managed to clip off to win for Kazakhstan. It was definitely a case of a hundred riders with a hundred stories and a hundred opportunities as we approached those final stages. You will know that I'm fond of describing sprints as a bit of a lottery . . . well, this race was like the euromillions. The only one of the big favorites to try to take the race to the home country was Spartacus himself, Fabian Cancellara, and his effort was short-lived when he misjudged a corner in Richmond Park and hit the deck.

The race was one thing. The Olympic experience was on a whole new level though, and not in the way you might think.

The road-race disciplines were the first events of the whole Games. While those of us who were involved were doing our best to prepare quietly and professionally, the Olympic Village was crammed, nearly bursting with excited young people. The opening ceremony was that same weekend—in fact, I think it was the night before our event—and as we prepared for the road race, we were surrounded by thousands of young athletes from across the world completely immersed in one of the most explosive nights of their lives. Outside of my bubble, I would have loved it. I would have been caught up in their joy and expectation. What a fantastic thing to happen to anybody. But it could never have been described as ideal preparation for one of the biggest events in a professional athlete's calendar.

So the Olympic Village was like a high school prom scene in a Hollywood movie. The air was thick with teenage hormones and, most incongruous of all for what is supposedly a paragon of modern sporting excellence, the heady scent of ten thousand Big Macs. The Games, and the Village, were sponsored by McDonald's. It was the Supersize Me Games. Crazy. I love visiting London, and one of the best things about the city is the quality and variety of the food available. Some of the best restaurants I've ever eaten in are in London, plus the general standard of snacks, supermarket fare, and even street food is great. Yet here I was living in a 24-hour drive-thru crammed with teenagers all trying to see how many McNuggets they could get in their mouths at one time.

I'm sure that when Marlon is a bit older I will love seeing his face when I tell him that I went to the Olympics in London, but frankly it was an experience that, on the whole, I was in no rush to repeat.

———

Rio 2016 was looming on the horizon. The road-race circuit featured a pretty significant climb that would seriously reduce my chances of winning. Another huge mark in the "cons" column was the memory of Cav's experience four years prior and the awareness that this time around it could well be me riding round and round with a hundred people on my wheel waiting for something to happen.

In the middle of what was beginning to feel like a pretty gloomy conversation with Gabriele and Lomba about all this stuff, we came up with what felt like a stroke of genius. Forget the Olympic Village. Forget the Olympic road race. We'd have a summer to remember chilling out on a Brazilian beach and do the mountain bike race instead. Yes, that's right, the Olympic mountain bike race. The chill atmosphere of MTB racing was something I hadn't experienced since I was a junior. And there was none of this ambiguity about how important the Olympics were to mountain biking. It's the daddy, pure and simple. Turn up, become a mountain biking legend, then disappear into the sunset, all in the space of one afternoon. Like the Lone Ranger. With Gabri as Tonto.

Why not? I love mountain biking. Come on, how hard could it be? Why so serious?

The first and biggest hurdle was getting Oleg Tinkov to agree to it. He was my boss, after all. He paid my wages. We knew by now that he was going to wind the team up at the end of 2016, but he wanted to be remembered, to be missed, and that meant going out with the biggest bang possible.

The shape of 2016 had been warped, as it often is in an Olympic year. The Games were to be held in August; then the Vuelta a España would straddle August and September, with the world's pushed right back to the middle of October. They were set to be held in Doha, and the extreme heat of the Gulf States in summer provided another reason for the event to be held so late in the calendar.

Long gone are the days where Jacques Anquetil or Bernard Hinault could turn up at Paris–Nice in the spring, and then race to win every week until the Tour of Lombardy in the autumn. There are many factors to explain this. Expectation is higher, even at the small races that used to be regarded as little more than training rides or exhibition events. The average speed of a stage on a Grand Tour has gone through the roof, largely because of the greater importance placed today on getting somebody into a break. In the twentieth century, the first hour of a long stage was a chance to chat with old friends in the peloton, catch up on the gossip, or work on your tan lines. Now this first hour is an insane free-for-all that takes place at the same sort of speed you'd expect in the last 20 kilometers of a stage, not the first.

Attention is so much higher now. Years ago there wouldn't have been any television coverage until the last hour of the biggest races and none at all at smaller ones. Apart from the Tour de France and the Monuments, the press corps could usually share a car to get from start to finish, and they'd be stopping for a decent roadside lunch too. Sean Yates told me stories of his first years in the peloton as a rider in the 1980s, when the entire team would hide in a village somewhere on a circuit and then rejoin the race as it approached its closing stages!

We shouldn't gloss over the fact that drugs in cycling have shaped the racing too. Yes, there were cheats at the top looking for the smallest advantage over their rivals, but there were dozens, maybe hundreds more, for whom illegal substances meant the difference between getting through the day or abandoning. I'm not going to suggest that the fight against drugs is won yet, but without doubt, the widespread use of drugs on an industrial scale thankfully ended before my days in the professional peloton, and you can see the difference in the shape of races. Look at races from the seventies, eighties, and the current decade, and you'll see something that had virtually disappeared in the 1990s and 2000s . . . you can see riders getting tired!

There is a new generation of directeurs sportifs and coaches in the sport who are also helping to clean up the sport. When Yates became a DS and rode with the team on a training ride, he was looked at as a curiosity by his car-driving peers, but as my career has progressed, riding with Yates, Patxi Villa, Steven de Jongh, and now Sylwester Szmyd has become the norm. The general consensus among these guys is that for their predecessors, once their career was done, no way would they want to go through all that again, whether they were taking illegal enhancements themselves or just trying to keep up with those who were. These guys love riding their bikes and are able to ride comfortably alongside their team in a way that suggests strongly that the sport is significantly cleaner than it was.

Anyway, I know I've gone off on a bit of a tangent, but what I'm trying to say is that you simply can't turn up at every race and expect to compete, and when your targets are as far apart as Gent–Wevelgem in March and the world's in October with the Tour of California, the Tour de France, and the Olympics or Vuelta thrown in, you have to plan your year with extreme care, or you get burnt out.

With this in mind, we went to Oleg with our plan. I don't think I've ever told anyone about this before, but what the hell, eh? Why so serious?

Hey Oleg, wouldn't it be cool to have the Olympic MTB champion on your team? Wow! History or what?

What Oleg wanted more than anything else was to end the season as the world's number 1 team. And the Olympic MTB race was not the place to pick up UCI road-ranking points. He wanted me at the Vuelta, which began in Galicia the day before the Olympic MTB race in Rio de Janeiro. That was a bit of a stretch.

Oleg, listen. I'm not going to be able to compete for the general classification at the Vuelta. It's got 10 summit finishes, the first of which is on stage 3, and stage 1 is a team time trial, so basically I'm not even within a shout of a few days in the leader's red jersey. In total, there are probably about four stages that I could seriously contend for. How many UCI points for a Vuelta stage win? Six. If it's UCI points we're hunting, it would be better to go to Canada again. Two proper WorldTour races, bags of UCI points. And much better preparation for Doha. The Vuelta is going to leave me exhausted, a month short of the world's.

He had a think about it. I knew there was going to be a bit of bargaining. That's how we do things. We can't just accept a proposition; there has to be negotiation. And that is what Oleg was bound to come back with.

"OK, Peter," began Oleg. "You can do the Olympic road race instead of the Vuelta."

"Oh, no, I don't want to do that. I've got no chance; it's too hilly. I might as well go to the Vuelta than do that."

More thinking.

"OK, this is the deal. You can do the Olympic MTB race. You can miss the Vuelta. But I want two Tour de France stage wins, two wins from the two Canadian races, and you do GP Plouay and the Eneco Tour."

The Eneco Tour was ideal prep for Doha, a week of good-quality racing in Belgium and Holland in late September. But Plouay? God, I hate that race. Brittany in September. Whenever I've visited, it's been like Glasgow in November. It's up and down all day in the wind and rain on a nasty circuit, and then you lose.

"Take it or leave it, Peter."

"I'll take it, Oleg."

We shook hands.

I had another little addition up my sleeve, but I wasn't going to tell Oleg about that just yet. I'd try to knock off the first part of his deal and then see how the scene was before I rocked the boat.

The Tour de France started in poignant fashion, with some similarities to the previous year's race. In 2016, the race was honoring the Normandy landings by visiting some of the beaches, and it began with the incredible spectacle of the peloton rolling away from Mont St. Michel, on the causeway that separates it from the rest of France. The similarities? Riders were falling off left, right, and center.

Unluckiest was Alberto. Despite Tinkoff doing everything right and keeping him near the front, despite his undoubted talent as a bike handler, he was a magnet for trouble in the first couple of days. Part of this thing about keeping your team leader at the front to keep him out of trouble is misleading. Yes, it's true, logic says that if there's a crash in the bunch some-where, the closer you are to the front, the less likely you are to be behind the stoppage. The statistics also show that the risk of losing time to crashes or other splits—crosswinds are always a gust away from causing problems in northern France—can be minimized by sitting closer to the front. However, if you've got, say, ten teams of nine riders trying to ride within the first 30 places all day, the mathematics dissolve pretty quickly. Ninety into thirty equals crashes.

On stage 1, Mark Cavendish showed that the speculation about his advancing years catching up with his speed were as premature as ever, and he flashed the rest of us a clean pair of heels. That made it nine years since his first Tour stage wins, sug-gesting that all this stuff about "burnout" affecting sprinters is subjective at best.

I'd been having a good look at stage 2 for a while, knowing that if I was to meet Oleg's target of two stage wins, I'd better pinpoint the ones that suited me best. I was also acutely aware that while I may have had four green jerseys hanging in my cupboard, I'd gone the last two Tours without winning a stage.

It was a disappointing finish for me. A break had been away all day, and with nervousness, crashes, and horrible weather affect-ing the bunch, we had misjudged catching them all, as they began to split ahead of us. In the last kilometer, Roman Kreuziger got on the front and put in a massive turn, catching Jasper Stuyven, one of the breakaways, in the last couple of hundred meters. I found myself in the front as we rose up the hill to the finish line with the likes of Alejandro Valverde and Julian Alaphilippe and the other uphill finishing specialists crowding on my wheel. Knowing this was a good opportunity to grab some green jersey points from Mark Cavendish, who was likely to finish farther back today, I led out along the barriers, but held back a little. Alaphilippe came around me and went eyeballs out for the line, but I'd stored enough that I was able to take his wheel as he came past me and then repass him at the top. It was good to win the sprint, just a shame it wasn't for the win.

Hang on. It normally takes quite a lot to get Gabri jumping up and down, but there he was, 50 meters past the line jumping up and down. He looks like a man who's fallen into a muddy ditch a lot of the time, but here he looked like a man who'd fallen into a muddy ditch and come out holding a winning lottery ticket. What? Had something happened to the people ahead of me on the classifications? Maybe I'd taken the green or even the yellow jersey?

I had taken the green and the yellow jersey. That was pretty good. But how I'd come to do it was a mystery until Gabri explained that Jasper Stuyven hadn't been left behind by the rest of the breakaway. He was the last of the breakaways; we'd already caught the others. Kreuziger's massive effort had set me up for the stage win, not the sprint for the minor placings. Come on!

I like jerseys. This rainbow one? It's pretty cool, and I will admit that I'm not going to enjoy watching somebody else wear it very much. I've also gotten used to that particular shade of green that you only see on the Tour de France's points jersey. But yellow? This was something new. Even people who've never seen a bike race in their lives know what the yellow jersey means. Some things are universally recognized by their color: Red Army. The blues. Black Sabbath. White wedding. Yellow jersey. And here I was on the podium of the Tour de France taking the prize for winning the stage in my rainbow jersey, covering that with the green jersey of points leader, then topping them all with the yellow jersey. Tour de France race leader. Not bad.

I wore that golden fleece for three memorable days, clocking up a couple more top-five finishes before passing it to my old sparring partner Greg Van Avermaet, who took it with a classy win after his breakaway group stayed away over some hilly roads in central France. After Cav took his third win of the race the next day, my green jersey disappeared as well. Never mind. I'd been missing those rainbow stripes, I told myself.

In all honesty, I knew that if the race went to form and I kept going well, the green was likely to come back to me. I wasn't the fastest flat-out sprinter in the race, but I could get up there when the flat-out guys couldn't. My target was another stage win. The green jersey would look after itself. So would the yellow, but if it didn't end up on Chris Froome's back, it certainly wouldn't end up on Peter Sagan's, and that was the truth. Tinkoff's yellow jersey hopes were looking pretty thin with Alberto's travails since the start, compounded by him getting sick at the end of the first week. When we hit the Pyrenees as the race entered its second week, it was clear that he wasn't going to make Paris, which was a shame for him and a final nail in the coffin for Oleg's hopes of winning a Tour de France. As consolation, I took back the green jersey from Cav when the road sloped up, and I was determined to make it the fifth time in five attempts that I would be wearing it on the Champs-Elysées podium.

I fancied the transitional stage that went east in the shadow of the Pyrenees from Carcassonne to Montpellier, stage 11. It ended up being one of the most talked-about stages of recent years, but neither I nor anybody else I know thought it would be beforehand. I knew that I would have a good chance if it came to the expected sprint. I'd been going well and came out of the mountains better than I had been while winning that stage and taking the jerseys in the first week. The Pyrenees had either weakened or removed some of the fast finishers, and I felt that this would be a stage that I could legitimately target.

All the talk all day was "Watch out for the crosswinds, look out, it's windy, yada yada yada." To be honest, it was fine. The promised wind didn't start rushing in off the Med until late in the day, probably the last 15 kilometers or so. Being keen on the finish, I'd made sure I was close to the front in case those winds led to a tired rider letting a wheel go here or there and echelons of riders battling gales starting to split and reform.

With 11 kilometers left, I felt pretty good and could feel the race stretching. The normal big arrowhead and following snake that you'd expect to see in the last 20 kilometers of a flat Tour stage just wasn't there. It was just a thinned-out long line of guys, not much teamwork, and I could see from the faces on show that nobody was enjoying it much.

I slipped up to the front of the line and put my head down. Maciej Bodnar was with me, and there is no better rider on any team that you would want with you at a moment like that, let alone one who had been a teammate for my entire professional career. Body saw what I was doing, and we went flat stick.

The team leader doing his job best, hanging out at the front of the race to avoid the splits that everybody was warning about, was the race leader, Chris Froome. He latched on, and at first, I thought he was trying to close me down, which would be fair enough. But a quick look and a word between us established that we had seen the same opportunity: "Let's do it."

Like me, he had a loyal teammate with him, Geraint Thomas, who was wise to the game. Between the four of us, we slipped into team time trial mode immediately. I thought to myself, "No way should we get caught: two Tinkoff, two Sky. One yellow jersey, one green jersey. Unusual? Yes. A good idea? No question."

We smashed it for 10 kilometers, the bunch panicking behind but not able to reel us in. The nature of crosswinds means you don't get as much protection in that arrowhead, so catching breaks isn't as easy as it would be on another stage. And when that break is comprised of the race leader, the points leader, and two of their strongest teammates . . . good luck.

Froomey was keen on a few seconds but also the stage winner's bonus seconds, so to his credit he decided to duke it out with me for the win, but I had enough to make it my second stage win, fulfilling part one of my Faustian pact with Oleg. We had a few seconds to spare on the gnashing teeth of the frustrated bunch sprint, but enough for my win to be comfortable and for Froomey to bag a bit more time on Quintana and his other rivals. They called it the most daring attack of modern times, which was bollocks. It was a chance, and when you see a chance, you have to try. That's how you win races. Chances come along in different ways, and you have to be alert to them: That's why a plan is only worth so much.

We clambered over Mont Ventoux. Fortunately for those of us not on such good terms with the high mountains as our skinny brethren, they shortened the stage, and we managed to miss the famous desert at the top because of high winds. Not quite so amusing for those G.C. guys though, as the effect of closing the final 6 kilometers of the most iconic mountainside in sport was to compress untold thousands of fans who had booked their entire summer holidays around that hour of excitement into the Forêt du Roland, on the lower slopes. As usual, the fans come last in the organizers' thoughts, but it was the riders, who usually run them a close second, who bore the brunt of the decision, when the race was physically stopped by the weight of people on the road and the press of motorcycles.

Motorcycles. Don't get me started. I'm in a good mood. Maybe I'll come back to them when I'm in a foul one.

Anyway, the brilliant but farcical sight of Froomey trying to run up cycling's most storied mountain in a pair of cycling shoes quickly relegated any other footage of the entire Tour to purely supporting features.

After beating me again a couple of days later in one of the only remaining sprint stages, Cav thoughtfully retired from the race to prep for that Olympic road race and missed the Alps that were beginning to loom large before we could make

Paris. Only after I'd managed to win my third stage though—bonus, Oleg!—in Switzerland. Still, he had four by then, and 30 in total. Thirty!

That Swiss stage win was memorable in its own way, just like all of them, I suppose. Cancellara was pumped up, as it was in his homeland, and he thought that with a few sprinters missing, this could be his day to take on the bunch. God knows he can shift at the end of a long hard race, so it was no real surprise. He probably didn't go for them more often because he had plenty of other ways to win and didn't need to get his hands dirty with us lot. On this occasion it looked like that strong bugger Alexander Kristoff had done for both Spartacus and me, not to mention the other hopefuls dashing for the line. However, on the day I seemed to just have a better idea than he did of where the line was, and when I threw my bike, my ass hanging way out over the back wheel, he was still sprinting, and I got it by less than the width of my tire.

It had been such a long hot day, 210 kilometers in absolutely sweltering conditions, and we did it in less than four and a half hours, which is pretty swift for a day like that in a race that was two and a half weeks old. There were two factors in that. The first was Tony Martin, who put in a monster long break that looked like giving him a beautiful solo win. But the second was my equally beautiful Team Tinkoff, who got on the front and drove the race into the ground in pursuit of Martin and to set it up for me.

There was added pressure and motivation for me, on top of the work my teammates had put in on my behalf. This is about as close as the Tour de France ever gets to Slovakia, and there were so many white, red, and blue flags and banners waving in the streets of Berne that I just couldn't let them down.

Alexander Kristoff is a really nice guy, and this wouldn't be the last time I put his nose out of joint, but what can I say? I like winning bike races. Sorry, Alexander. I believe in God, I believe in destiny, and I believe in balance. After all the narrow second places I'd endured in the last few years at the Tour and elsewhere, maybe the seesaw was just beginning to edge back up my way? Until Sunday, anyway, when Andre Greipel beat me by about the same margin on the Champs-Elysées. *C'est la vie.* And come on, Peter, three stage wins and that green jersey that is your July color of choice. Why so serious, man?

So. Operation Rio was greenlit. Gabriele and I packed our bags and flew to Park City, Utah. Until now, the summer of 2016 had been hot, hard, and fun. For the next few weeks, it was going to be hot and fun but only as hard as we wanted it to be.

I didn't get those four hundred miles of trails in Park City all to myself though. No. There was a new contender on the horizon.

A man for whom no obstacle was too great, no mountain too high, no descent too frightening. Who was this superhero? Surely not Gabriele, the mild-mannered manager . . . on an electric bike.

I couldn't shake him off. I'd blast up a hill in the thin Utah atmosphere, and there he'd be, grinning from ear to ear.

Those few weeks . . . it was like I was 18 in Žilina again. Magical. We'd concocted this plan because it seemed like fun, but here I was, chock-full to the gills of the first new motivation I'd had in seven years. Don't get me wrong, I love road racing. It's the life I've chosen, and it's been amazing to me. But the calendar leaves your life prescribed. Press conferences bring the same dull questions every day. You remember the streets, the corners, and the hills, and your successes or your failures just drive you to do it again and do it better each time. But this was different. It was new, and I hadn't done "new" for a long time.

By the time we were jetting to Rio, I was as pumped as I'd ever been. Bouncing off the walls. Remembering the booming midnight music coming through the paper-thin walls of the London Olympic Village, sharing a room with young guys you've never met and the constant efforts of boy trying to meet girl, Giovanni, Gabriele, and Specialized had shunned the Rio Olympic equivalent and come up trumps. We had a beautiful apartment to ourselves on the beach. Every night we put our feet up, drank fresh coconut water straight from the shell, and reminded ourselves just how bloody lucky we were.

A few weeks ahead of the Games, we hooked up with Christoph Sauser. If you're reading this, you're probably a roadie and don't know who Christoph is. Take it from me: The man is an MTB legend. Hailing from Switzerland, he won a medal at the Sydney Olympics, was world champion in 2008, and best of all won the aptly named Cape Epic in South Africa no fewer than five times. He has retired—a couple of times, like George Foreman or Frank Sinatra—since then, but the man is still a mean rider. Above and beyond all that, he is Mr. Specialized when it comes to mountain biking, and my bike suppliers were pulling out all the stops to help me in Rio. Thank you, Specialized: Riding with Christoph wasn't just useful; it was bloody brilliant.

Christoph was pleased with how little pace I'd lost over my years away from the fat tires, and it was true, each ride was like going from beginner to expert in an hour. Brilliant fun. I'd wobble and dab my foot in the first couple of corners, then on the way back down I'd be sliding sideways down a huge scree slope with 100 percent control. I'd race round the banked planks of north shore corners with 10-meter drops on either side like I was descending the Poggio.

The papers in Slovakia ran stories about how I was getting showy. Too important to slum it with the man on the street anymore. Fame had gone to my head, and money had changed me. You know what? They were right. Money had changed me. It had given me responsibility, and it had given me the means and the desire to do things right. I owed it to everybody who had helped me—with money, frequently—to do my best to fulfill the promise they'd seen in me. And if that meant not sharing a frat house with dozens of teenagers bursting with testosterone, estrogen, rave music, and McFlurries, then that wasn't the worst plan I could come up with.

I kicked Gabri's sorry ass at FIFA on the PS4 every single night. He paid for dinner every night as a result, so don't take any of that rubbish he spins about letting me win for the sake of my morale. That might wash sometimes, but not when putting his hand in his pocket is the price. Not every night. Not the Gabriele I know.

Race time. The circuit was fun but tricky. It was also really hard to overtake someone, a bit like Formula One. Technical, narrow, with loads of obstacles that required total concentration, certainly not things that you could ignore while trying to pass another guy. It was fun because of the tricks you had to pull, and amusing stuff like sand traps in the shape of Havaianas flip-flops.

Another Formula One similarity was the starting grid, and this was my first and most serious problem. Not being a regular

MTB racer, I had no form and no points to give me a good start position. If it had really been like F1, we could have turned the whole race into a week's worth of testing and qualifying, but we're obviously not as savvy as those crafty media manipulators in motor racing, and I had to start where my nonexistent world ranking said I should be. At the back.

When I say the back, stone-cold last would give you the most accurate picture. There were 50 guys between me and the start line. By the time I crossed it, the clock would have been ticking, wheels spinning, people cheering, and the front riders disappearing into the middle distance. Sounds bad? If it had been a World Cup race, there might have been as many as 200 guys separating me from my clear destiny as Olympic MTB champion.

The first section of the lap was inside the stadium they had built to give spectators the best view. There were some backward-and-forward sections, a bit like the line at airport security, but it was wide and fast, unlike the course proper. I knew that once the stadium was behind us, overtaking someone would be a hundred times more difficult than in that first 60 seconds of a one-and-a-half-hour race.

For one of the first occasions in my career, I had a plan. As we lined up, each guy wiggling a little bit to get the best position, but kept in line by the officials trying to keep it fair, I went the other way. I backed up about 3 meters behind the penultimate line of riders. With the other 50-odd starters wedged into a 5-meter space, I looked ridiculous. I imagined them snickering at the dickhead roadie who was scared of getting knocked off in the free-for-all. The countdown started at 10. At five, I clicked into my right pedal. At three, I set off, clicking into the other pedal and going hell-for-leather through the startled lines of those patiently waiting. I thought: It can't be a false start. I haven't crossed the start line, right?

After three turns of the stadium, I was in third place. The guys who started on the front of the grid were in about 20th. I don't know much about MTB racing, it's true, so I'm ready for somebody to explain to me some day what their strategy was.

Mine was clear. Relax. Take it easy. There were seven laps ahead of us, and the first one would be the fastest. Breathe, see how it's going, don't kill yourself. Follow the wheel of somebody good—if he was second in the Olympic MTB race, he was probably pretty decent—and see how the pros do it. It'll open up later. And the last time I had to fight for the finish of an important race after an hour and a half, I'd probably been about 15. I reckoned that if it came to a late fight on the last lap, I'd back myself to have something left in the tank. Stay in contention. As José Mourinho would say: Stay in the game.

Lap 1 went pretty well. I went through the pits and gave my guys a confident nod. That would be the last time that day that anything went well.

Immediately after the pits, I got a tricky section wrong and totally shredded my front tire on some big sharp rocks. Mountain bike racing comes from a long history of self-sufficiency. In my junior days, we'd hear stories of professionals stuffing grass into their tires to fix punctures or finishing races with only one side of their handlebars. The legacy of this proud tradition is that you're not allowed service or outside help on the circuit except at the two designated pit areas. And you're not allowed to go backward. Shit.

I ran half a lap with a flat front tire. You know that old joke about your tire only being flat at the bottom? Well, mine wasn't. It was flapping about like a seagull with a broken wing. So I ran like a Muppet for about two and a half kilometers to reach the other pit area. During that time, I discovered that it was actually quite easy to overtake someone out on the circuit after all. Just make sure he was the Slovakian bloke pushing his bike while everybody else is riding theirs.

I hopped back on occasionally and jumped off when it got bumpy. It was properly messed up when I got my new wheel, and I was relieved to feel like a cyclist rather than a moronic street entertainer again. I was in about 20th, I guessed. I faced up to the reality that it was unlikely that the 19 or so men in front of me were all bad enough to get caught by me but thought that I could maybe make the top 10 and regain some dignity.

I got back up to the top 10 and breathed hard. Not so bad. Let's see how high we can go. I went through the pits and gave them another nod. And then I flatted again!

This one was really annoying and totally avoidable. It was a slow puncture in the rear, and it dawned on me agonizingly that I'd actually sustained it before the pits. If I'd been a bit more on the ball, I could have had a bike swap in seconds. As it was, I was back to running for another delightful half a lap.

Have you ever run in mountain bike shoes? The cleat is recessed into the sole to allow you to walk about in them, whether you've punctured at the Olympics, need to climb over a gate, or just go into the café for a slice of cake. Running is another matter as there is no flex in the sole whatsoever. You can't spring like in running shoes, your heel rubs like crazy as your foot bends but the shoe doesn't, and there's always a good chance of twisting your ankle on a rock. I was just thinking that when I twisted my ankle on a rock.

I finished 35th, a lap behind the winner and Christoph's countryman, Nino Schurter.

For five minutes I was spitting mad. Gabri knows better than to come near me when I'm angry. Better than that, he knows to keep everybody else away too, and for that I am always grateful. He's always a good friend, but great friends are there when you need them most, and that's him. But after that five minutes, I had a sudden memory of the look on all of the other riders' faces at the start when I began charging through them all after my starting run-up. I couldn't help but laugh.

People said I was unlucky, but mountain bikers know that punctures aren't luck, they're things you need to be a good enough bike rider to avoid if you want to win races. And I hadn't been good enough. Strong enough? Maybe, maybe not, but it's immaterial. You don't win races just by being strong, otherwise it would be Body, Burghardt, Giovanni, or Yates sitting here telling you about their rainbow jerseys. You've got to be strong, sure, but there's other stuff you need, and in Rio I didn't have it.

So it wasn't my destiny to be Olympic mountain bike champion after all. But we had a bloody good laugh.

———

Back on the coast, I was watching TV and suddenly up pops Greg Van Avermaet, Olympic road race champion. Holy shit! Greg won the road race! And it was days ago; I'd been so wrapped up in myself that I hadn't even thought about it. Gabriele and

Giovanni had sad smiles on their faces. They'd known but didn't want to tell me. They thought that if I'd seen GVA had won, then I would have felt that maybe I could have beaten him, that maybe it wasn't a climber's race after all. Jesus. That didn't bother me in the slightest. What bothered me was that Greg had been Olympic road race champion for two weeks, and I hadn't called him to congratulate him. He must have thought I was a proper dick.

AUTUMN

There was only a week between the Olympic mountain bike race and Plouay, so we found ourselves somewhat hastily on a flight back across the Atlantic. I had plenty of time to reflect on the Rio experience.

My thoughts inevitably wandered to the Olympic road race, now that I'd heard how it all panned out. Had Gabriele and Giovanni been justified in worrying that I would think I'd made a mistake in not riding it?

I weighed it up. From what I could see, Vincenzo Nibali had been the race's true animator, and his crash on what had proved to be a genuinely dangerous circuit was the day's pivotal moment. He fell with Sergio Henao, another climber with medal aspirations, and Richie Porte had gone the same way a bit earlier. The race was turned on its head, and Greg Van Avermaet had ridden such a strong race that he was able to grab it by the scruff of the neck and become Olympic champion, a truly remarkable ride by any standards.

Would it have been different if I'd been there? Of course it would have. Not because of my presence, but because no two races are ever the same. Nibali hardly ever crashes. Even then, Henao is strong enough to go alone, but he also went down. If the chasers include Greg and me, nobody else is going to work with us to bring it back. Basically, it's the old hundred riders with a hundred stories narrative, all taking place on a course that nobody's used to racing on that can throw you head first into a tree at 90 kph. Greg is the Olympic champion, should be the Olympic champion, and that's it.

That got me thinking about cycling more generally and what we go through.

In the women's race, Annemiek van Vleuten was soloing to what looked like a certain gold, when the horrible Vista Chinesa descent put paid to her dreams and very nearly a lot more. That she was at trackside the next day was simply unbelievable for many people who'd seen her hit the road with such a sickening impact and feared the worst. Cycling, eh? I was following the women's Liège–Bastogne–Liège and saw Marianne Vos when she needed a plate and screws inserted in her shoulder after a crash there. She finished the race, though. What a hard-core bunch we are.

———

I went straight to Plouay, a small village in the heartlands of French cycling, Brittany. Bernard Hinault is the epitome of a Breton cyclist: proud, strong, and indomitable. Despite the unpretentious surroundings and its many incarnations—I think it was officially called the GP Bretagne Ouest France in 2016— the race is universally known for the host village. They had the world championships here in 2000. It rained.

In 2016 it rained, too, but not all day. What goes on all day is that you spend six hours climbing and descending on country lanes in showers and gales on a twisty circuit until you can't work out whether you're coming or going.

Except that I wasn't coming or going. I was sick. Totally empty with my head spinning, wobbling all over the road. I abandoned after 50 kilometers. I should really have just missed it all together and gone directly to Monaco, but I had promised Oleg, and that mattered to me. Plus, my credit on the Faustian pact that a green jersey and three Tour stages had bought me had now been wiped out by my Olympics flop.

The next part of the deal was two wins in the two Canadian WorldTour races. The first was 12 days away. I lay in bed in Monaco for a week, sweating and puking. I don't get sick often, but when I do, it's usually at this time of year. Holding form from the cold northern spring through the three weeks of the Tour at the height of the summer is hard, but if you go on racing afterward, especially if it involves a lot of travel, your card is marked. Coming back to a cold wet Europe from tropical South America when your system is depleted is always going to be a risk. Anyway, it is what it is. I spent a week off the bike. Unheard of. When I surfaced the following Monday, Sylwester and Oscar Gatto, my neighbor in Monaco, persuaded me to get the Monaco MTB out of the garage and trundle around a little bit of the Riviera with them. It was horrible. I was so weak. And I was meant to be winning a race on the other side of the Atlantic on Friday.

Sylwester said: "Just finish. Oleg won't be disappointed if you go over there and do your best for the team and the jersey." Yeah, I thought, but "just finishing" isn't straightforward when it's 200 kilometers over a tricky little circuit with riders desperately chasing WorldTour ranking points and Michael Matthews, Tom Boonen, and GVA are all using it as a dry run for the world's. I'll go with "just fly out there." Then I'll maybe stretch to "just start." And then we'll see how close we get to "just finish."

I like Canada. It has a very chill vibe, with nothing to prove. Québec City is the most European city outside of Europe that I've ever been to, so I felt totally at ease there. We flew in on Wednesday and spent Thursday meeting the press and doing as little as possible. I felt like shit, so I just got the bike out to check that it was working, really. My legs certainly weren't.

Fortunately, Friday was a lovely day, and I got through the "just start" part of the equation a bit creakily but acceptably. A break of eight went away, and the race settled down. You know what? I started to feel all right. I ate more on the bike than I had at home for a week. The pedals started turning in ever-smoother circles. With 15 kilometers to go, I surprised myself by riding up to the front of the race and thinking . . . *I reckon I could do something here.*

Oleg's drive for the top spot meant that we'd traveled with a really strong Tinkoff team. Oscar had come with me from Monaco, and there was an engine room with Body, Kreuziger, and Kolář stomping away. To their surprise, I gave them the nod, and they began to exert their power on the sharp end of the race. I didn't know at the time, but the 2016 Grand Prix Cycliste de Québec was going to be one of the most exciting finishes I'd been involved in.

There were little moves forming and coming back off the front, but when Gianni Moscon slipped off with a Quick-Step duo, it looked very dangerous. I gambled on not going as hard as possible on the last lap, as I knew the straight to the line was hard and into the wind. It wasn't a dissimilar finish to the world's circuit at Richmond, but I thought that it would be hard to stay away in that breeze. Rigoberto Urán was the defending champion, and he launched one of those trademark slow wind-up moves near the top of the climb, passed the Quick-Step guys, went round Moscon, and lined up the drag to the line. Watching it now on YouTube, it's hard to believe that with 200 meters to go, he could lose. But that finish is really, really hard, and suddenly you see the pack slip into the picture.

As you know, in a headwind sprint, my aim is always to stay covered up for as long as possible. But that wasn't going to work today, because Anthony Roux was sprinting all out into that wind, and I was worried that he wasn't going to catch Urán. I came off his wheel with Greg Van Avermaet on mine earlier than I wanted, but this was one day that had just got better and better the longer it had gone on. I passed Urán with a few meters to go, and Greg just couldn't get around me. Outgoing world champion first, incoming Olympic champion second. That's a good race.

It was the same one-two on Sunday in Montreal on a slightly hillier circuit where I'd won previously in 2013. The same one-two? Oh, OK. Same one-two, but different order. Incoming Olympic champion first, outgoing world champion second. Nice ride, GVA.

I like a special jersey. It's cool. Since my second season as a pro, when I won the Slovakian national road race title for the first time, I've been entitled to have my own jersey, first as Slovakian champion, then world champion. It's great to step up onto a podium and wear a leader's jersey in a race or classification, but there is no downside to giving it back because I return to my own champion's jersey, and people know who I am. A friend worked out recently that since I turned professional, I've only spent 20 percent of all my racing days in a straightforward team jersey. Call me proud, call me conceited, but what the hell, I think it's cool.

In 2016 at the Slovakian national road race, I was proud for a different reason: Juraj won for the first time. Now we had the world champion's jersey and the national champion's jersey alongside each other at both the family home and Tinkoff. Since my win in Richmond, my national champion's jersey hadn't been seen in public as I obviously had to wear the rainbow stripes, so I was delighted for Juraj and for Tinkoff, but also for Slovakia, as the colors were flying again.

It did lead me to a slightly darker thought though. When my year in the rainbow stripes was up, I would be going back to the ranks. OK, I will be able to wear the rainbow collar and cuffs of former world champion on any jersey I wear for the rest of my career, and that's pretty good. But there're a lot of former world champions out there—BMC had virtually a whole team of them at one time!—but only one world champion. My brother already had the Slovakian jersey. There would be nothing for Peter except a good old-fashioned team strip.

There was something I could do. I hadn't told Oleg (remember I'd kept something up my sleeve after our pact?), but in 2016 there was going to be the inaugural running of the European road championships. I didn't know who would be going or how hard it would be, but I knew something . . . it was going to have a jersey. And there is always room in my wardrobe for more jerseys. I had until October before I had to go to Doha and give back the rainbow jersey that was beginning to fade with all the washing it had been getting. Then I would be able to prance around for the whole of 2017 in the white with blue bands that the first professional European champion would be awarded. It was going to be held in my home town, too. Monaco and Nice would host a five-day cycling festival with the climax being the elite road race on Sunday afternoon. It would be rude not to compete on my own doorstep, and it would be cool to be working and at home at the same time for once.

Remember that thing about plans being good but unreliable? Terror struck the town neighboring my own in July while we were away at the Tour. A monster claiming to represent an ideological cause decided that the best way to aid that cause would be to drive a truck into a crowd on the Promenade des Anglais in Nice and end the lives of 86 happy people enjoying the Bastille Day holiday, ironically the day France celebrates the freedom of the individual. Countless more people had their lives changed forever through injury, fear, or bereavement.

Apart from leaving a black cloud hanging over all of us, the most pertinent effect on me was a comparatively mundane one: The European championships were no longer to be held in Monaco and Nice.

They were moved north, to be held on the course of the annual Coupe de France event, the GP Plumelec in Brittany, just a few miles from my least favorite race, Plouay.

As it turned out, there was a really powerful lineup. Most national federations were using the event as prep for the forthcoming world's and wanted to replicate the teams and setup as closely as possible.

Now. Here was my problem. I'd promised Oleg that I would ride the Eneco Tour in the low countries. I'd also promised him two wins in Canada. I'd come back with a win and a second place from the two races, which was pretty good, but didn't leave me in a position to back out of anything else. I'd kept pretty quiet about the European championships, but there was the fact that the road race was on Sunday afternoon in western France and the Eneco began on Monday morning in the Netherlands, 1,100 kilometers away.

I raised it gently with Oleg. Oleg . . . umm . . . I think this new European championships road race would be a great thing for us to win. But it clashes with Eneco. Umm . . . maybe . . . perhaps . . . ?

No way. Not only was the Euros a national team event, so no Tinkoff jerseys in the race, he wouldn't even reap the benefit of seeing Tinkoff on any jersey if I won, because I was still wearing the rainbow jersey until Qatar, and that's when the team would wind up. On the other hand, Eneco was a race well suited to the team, to me, and had a fistful of late WorldTour points on offer.

Fair enough. I could see his logic and, as we've established, he paid the bills.

However, he had only demanded that I do Eneco. He hadn't said I couldn't ride the Euros.

––––––

Plumelec is a small town with a nasty little hill in the middle of it. I rode up it more times than I care to remember that day, as a 13-kilometer circuit was used to stage a 232-kilometer race. I'll let you work it out—I don't want to think about it any more than I absolutely have to. Each time we went over the top of the Côte de Cadoudal, there were fewer of us left, until, approaching 4:00 p.m., I gave it my full effort for the final 100 meters and outsprinted Julian Alaphilippe to become the first professional European champion. Yes!

The jersey was nice. It was white, with three blue bands of gradually darkening hue, speckled with some random yellow stars. Google me in it, and you'll see me wearing it for 30 seconds on the podium in Plumelec. That remains the only 30 seconds that I've ever worn it.

Gabriele and Giovanni were waiting behind the podium with the engine running and my bike in the trunk. I jumped in wearing my full kit—it had been a nice day, thankfully—and Gabri floored it to the nearest airfield. I remember that they wouldn't even let me stop for a piss and a Tinkoff water bottle had to do the job while he drove.

There was a little plane waiting for me on the runway, and that too had the engine running. I'd paid for it myself—asking Oleg or the national federation would have been taking the piss without the need of a Tinkoff bottle. I hopped on board, and we rose into the darkening eastern sky. Far below, I watched Gabriele heading the same way in the car with my bikes and kit. See you tomorrow, my friend.

I met the Tinkoff guys in Holland late that night and slept the kind of sleep that only a newly crowned European champion can sleep. Thankfully, stage 1 of the Eneco Tour didn't begin until a generous 11:00 a.m., so I had a reasonable amount of time in bed. A lot more than Gabriele . . . the legend turned up at 9:00 a.m. looking even more disheveled than usual. I know he claims to be Italian, but looks can be deceptive. To be fair to the great man, he had spent the entire night behind the wheel to keep the pact

alive. I already owed him a lot; now it was going to take something special to repay him.

It's stories like this that remind you how uniquely crazy
cycling is among the pantheon of professional sports. It's like a
camping trip. There are no stadiums, arenas, courses, theaters, or
racetracks as in any other global sport you can name. Everything
moves every day. Even in other sports where they trot around
like a traveling circus, they know where they're going. F1 loads
up its trucks and planes but turns up at Spa or the Nürbur-
gring or Silverstone year in, year out. Jockeys use planes and
helicopters to go to three meetings in a day, but when they get
there, the track will be familiar. In cycling, you might not even
know where the finish line is going to be. Are there corners? Are
there hills? How steep are they? Is it narrow? Which way does
the wind blow? On the start line of the world's once, a journalist
asked me if I'd scouted the course. I did that thing where I look
at him for a moment before answering. "I'm going to ride across
that finish line 12 times between now and the finish. That'll be 12
times more than I've ever scouted the route of one of my Tour de
France wins. I'll figure it out somehow."

There was one other little story from that funny day in
Plumelec. It occurred about halfway through the race when I
was clearly fed up.

Ján Valach had called Gabriele at the finish line from the team car.

"Gabri, we have a problem."

"What?"

"Peter doesn't want to finish the race. He wants to pack it in and go to Holland now."

"OK, don't worry, I have the answer. Kill Peter. No, tell him that if he doesn't finish, in fact, if he doesn't win, I promise to strangle him myself with my bare hands. I haven't signed up to drive 15 hours through the night just to watch him pack in, halfway through."

"Thanks, Gabri, I'll tell him."

After my dip in health between Brazil and Canada, I was miraculously mining a rich vein of form now. First in Québec City, second in Montreal, and first in Plumelec were followed by two stages and third overall at the Eneco Tour. Considering that there were two time trials among the seven stages, I thought that was pretty good. I don't know how much of it Gabriele remembers. He was asleep all week.

Oleg, on the other hand, was delighted. I was now the owner of an unassailable lead in the UCI WorldTour standings and Tinkoff would end its final season in the peloton with the World-Tour No. 1 ranked rider and world champion. Oleg and I had not seen eye to eye for every minute of every day that we had been together, but my God, he's missed. A massive character with massive passion for the game and we want him back someday.

Of the 13 wins I'd had in 2016, 10 of them were on the World-Tour, and I'd first taken the lead in the standings after winning Gent–Wevelgem in March. Alberto, and then Nairo Quintana, had temporarily topped the rankings in the summer with the long tours throwing up plenty of points, but my flourish at the end of the year had put me back on the top step. I dedicated the award to Oleg and the Tinkoff team. It was in no way a solo achievement.

And now there was just one last race to do. My year in rainbow stripes had been one I'd never forget. I wanted it to end in style.

"If a world championships takes place in the desert and nobody is around to see it, has the world championships really taken place?" wondered *Cyclingnews* in Doha. You could see their point. There was nobody about. It was like a building site where the job is basically finished, but it's the weekend, and the grand opening isn't until Monday. Or one of those car commercials, where a car looking much the same as the ones in the other car commercials races through empty streets past pristine buildings in never-ending yellow sunshine. Welcome to Doha. Here are the buildings, here are the steeples, open the doors: Where are all the people?

On the plus side, the impressive few dozen people who'd traveled from Slovakia to support me found themselves, by default, the largest and loudest band of supporters at the whole event.

To go with the deathly atmosphere, the race itself was intensely dull.

For once, I felt pretty sorry for the press pack. They were trying to whip up some kind of intrigue or intensity as usual, but there was absolutely nothing for them to work with. Here we were in a deserted desert city, the scarcely seen inhabitants oblivious to our presence, a circuit with nothing but sun, sand, and wind to define it. Low point: zero meters above sea level. High point: zero meters above sea level. The equivalent of Alpe d'Huez, Arenberg, or the Angliru was essentially a flyover.

I didn't arrive until three days before the race, while the press pack and plenty of the riders had already been there for a week. It was like a gang of ducks on a pond hoping that you're going to throw them some bread, even though you've never thrown them any bread before and you're clearly not carrying any bread.

"Peter, are you hoping it will be fast from the start, and it breaks up early? Please don't say, 'We will see on Sunday.'"

"Ah. I was going to say, 'We will see on Sunday.' Sorry."

"Peter, do you feel under pressure as reigning champion to win on Sunday?"

"No. I've won it already. There's less pressure on me. What do I have to lose?"

"A rainbow jersey?"

"I already have one of those."

There had been so much talk about the heat, about how late it was in the season, about the need to acclimatize. I looked at it like this: The season's done. This is a one-off outside that. Like a Christmas party or a holiday romance. I just wanted to be at home. I'd been away all year. Go home, chill out, ride normally, arrive as late as possible. Giovanni told me to put my turbo trainer in the sauna and crank up the watts. Jesus, Lomba, it's meant to be fun. Why so serious?

Out in the desert on the opening remote part of the *parcours*, the wind blew. Everybody knew that the wind would blow, but somehow, some people with actual designs on winning the race were taken by surprise and found themselves out of contention with 180 kilometers left to race. Bear in mind that most races aren't even as long as that; this was the biggest target of the second half of the season, and anybody in the race had gone through a grueling selection one way or another to be here. Underestimating the conditions was almost criminally negligent.

I was pretty sure even then that it would come down to a sprint. There wasn't much point in attacking on a flat, windy, featureless circuit. There were plenty of fast guys left, but at least we would be spared the mess of 10 teams and 10 long lead-out trains. I reckoned I would probably get top 10 and maybe my old maxim of aiming to make the top five in any sprint would be within my grasp. Beyond that? You know what I'm going to say. Any sprint is a lottery.

I had a teammate with me, Michal Kolář. He was only 23, strong as an ox, and a teammate all year round because he was Tinkoff and Slovak. Young, but no novice, after doing a sterling ride at Richmond a year before. I knew I could rely on him at the death, but there was little work needed earlier on, as Daniele Bennati pulled all day on the front for his Italian teammates, Elia Viviani and Giacomo Nizzolo. Mark Cavendish had Adam Blythe with him for GB and the two of them had obviously also decided that it was going to be a sprint and therefore their day. They were glued to my rear wheel like two red, white, and blue shadows for 100 kilometers. Tom Boonen and GVA were there with Belgian support riders. Kristoff and Boasson Hagen were there wishing the weather was a bit more Norwegian, as were Michael Matthews and William Bonnet. So there was an awful lot of speed left, even if the numbers were low. It was a shame we couldn't just forget 150 kilometers of deathly boring bike riding in an oven in front of a crowd of none and just cut straight to the sprint that we'd all tacitly agreed on.

The Belgian and Italian squads are two of those who have seen their chances at many world's wrecked by internal rivalries, but these are different times, and, more importantly, Tom, Greg, and the Italians are nicer guys than their noxious, preening predecessors who would rather lose to another country than see a rival teammate win.

Being from a smaller nation, I've never had that sort of worry. In fact, on this day, I was so relaxed, and with so little to prove that I looked at Michal Kolář and felt a whole different pride run through me. "Michal," I said to him, "this is your time. You can win this. I've got one already. They'll all be looking at me. I'll lead you out. It's yours to take."

It was unfair of me. Michal was reveling in his role as final teammate of the world champion. He was ready to bury himself to help me win again. He wasn't ready to win himself, and certainly not when he looked around and saw Cav, Tom, Greg, Viviani, and Kristoff all grimly focused on their own version of the hundred different stories. I'd just made it 101 stories without serious consideration.

I heard later that Ján Valach had called Gabriele at the finish from the team car.

"Gabri, we have a problem."

"What?"

"Peter doesn't want to sprint. He wants to lead Kolář out instead."

"OK, don't worry, I have the answer. Kill Peter. No, wait, kill Michal Kolář. No, wait, just kill both of them."

Michal was actually pretty tired and was worried that he was faltering in the heat in the last 20 kilometers. He did what was by far the most useful thing he could have done in the circumstances. He took himself to the front of the race in front of all those champions and ground himself into the swirling, sizzling dust with every last scrap of effort he had left, knowing that if we didn't keep the pace high, some chancer would launch a late move to draw the sting of the sprinters.

Kolář's turn was immense, and I won't forget it in a hurry. I remember grinning to myself in wonder like a proud uncle. Pull yourself together, Peter, you're only 26 yourself! To be honest, the whole race was so forgettable that I'm sitting here now watching it on YouTube with Gabri and Lomba, and it's like seeing it for the first time. I can hardly recall being there, just that sauna heat in your nostrils and dust in your mouth.

Look at that, the Dutch guy Tom Leezer has launched a really good attack. He means it. I remember that somebody went, but I thought it was Terpstra. He was out of sight from my position in the line, but I knew it was going to be a close thing if we were going to catch him. Seeing it later, I find it unfathomable that he isn't following the racing line. Every time they show him, he's on the wrong side of the road or going all the long way around the outside of a bend. It could have been even closer.

The sprint opens up as he is caught, Tom dominating for Belgium, Nizzolo representing the Italians. I go right, seeing a gap on the rail. Adam Blythe delivers a perfect lead for Cav, but the Manx Missile hesitates for a fraction of a second, perhaps remembering that he'd decided that it was my wheel he was going to follow. He starts to do just that, then flicks back left to try to pass Boonen on his other side. But his race is lost. I have hit the front at the perfect moment and feel it is mine. I know it is mine.

That was some podium. Me, Cav, and Tom. The world champion from 2015, the world champion from 2011, and the world champion from 2005. Great podium, shame about the race.

Gabriele was going berserk. He was so sure I'd win; he had been all year. Bless his heart. Some bets and challenges would be paid off now, and it would be a delicious payday, no matter what the expense. As we waited for the podium, he and I watched the replay of the finale in the press area, and they were playing it with the English commentary. It went something like: "Cavendish! Cavendish! Cavendish! Oh . . . Sagan." Gabriele was wetting himself.

I will be in the rainbow jersey for another 12 months. Sorry, Euros. It's the wardrobe for you.

PART THREE

Bergen

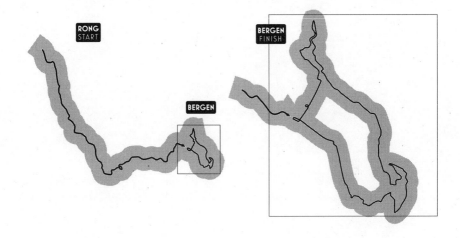

On BORA-hansgrohe

At the end of 2015, Oleg Tinkov announced that he was going to step away from the sport at the end of the following season. To say the announcement took us by surprise would be a whopping understatement. We knew that he had been at the center of a largely unsuccessful and frustrating drive to reduce cycling's dependency on sponsorship, but I don't think anyone had realized he was ready to step away from the sport altogether. Colorful as ever, he said he felt like Don Quixote tilting at windmills, and I have to say that when he sat us all down to break the news, I did feel a tinge of sympathy for him. Securing funding for our sport can be a real scrap, and perhaps the system does need an overhaul. But the sport also clings to its traditions, and I'm certain we'd need a few more Olegs all pulling in the same direction before we witness a noticeable improvement.

Any kind of abrupt change can be alarming, but I could immediately tell that Lomba saw an opportunity. He quickly settled my nerves and reassured me that the outcome would be positive, and of course I entirely trusted him. When had he ever let me down? However, I couldn't help but feel anxious for both Juraj and the rest of my teammates. Yes, I was UCI World Champion, but I could still appreciate the stress they must have been feeling. I came up through the haphazard Slovakian system, remember!

The responsibility of pitching for a new owner and sponsor fell to team manager Stefano Feltrin, with whom Lomba had a testy relationship over the years. The idea of dancing to his tune was distinctly unappealing.

And so as the 2016 season rolled on, various opportunities and outcomes were explored and scrutinized. We wrote up a short list of attributes a new team needed in order to appeal to us and decided that a key factor would be ensuring that I had the freedom to listen to my body and race the events that would be best for my career. It seemed more important than ever that I was able to take control of my racing schedule if I was going to peak at the right times. God knows I'd had enough battles with Oleg already about our conflicting objectives. They were distracting, and hopefully they wouldn't be a feature of my future team. I was also looking for a team manager who understood the important role of Team Peter and had a vision for how our compact, focused unit could integrate into a larger team for the benefit of all. What else? A level of professionalism and long-term stability that meant I could focus on riding, the opportunity to bring over Juraj, and some of my ever-dependable teammates, oh, and the moon on a stick, perhaps?

There were mentions of several large teams, but somehow joining one of the bigger outfits felt like a step backward. Could I realistically expect to avoid wrestling over race schedules and goals when there were other top riders with their own opposing ambitions on the same bus?

It was at this point that an exciting, refreshing opportunity came into view. At that time, BORA–Argon 18 was a relatively small team with grand ambitions. They were riding under a pro-continental license but were set for the top tier in 2017. We met with founder and CEO of BORA, Willi Bruckbauer, and team manager, Ralph Denk. They were instrumental in guiding me to make one of the best decisions of my professional career. To give you a little background, BORA is a German company that specializes in sophisticated kitchen exhaust systems, which means you can do away with those big hoods you have looming over your stove. Much like Oleg, Willi is a cycling fanatic who wanted to get into the sport to expand his company brand, although I think it's safe to say that's where their similarities end. He is passionate, but thoughtful and precise. Anyone can grab a microphone and make absurd claims about taking their team to the top of the sport, but Willi and Ralph had such a clear strategy, and they wanted to position me at the heart of it. They listened to us intently and seemed unfazed when we stated our desire to keep Team Peter together, which would mean bringing in Tinkoff teammates Maciej Bodnar, Michal Kolář, Erik Baška—and Juraj obviously—to the team as well. For the first time I began to visualize the role as a true team leader.

Willi was also in the process of signing a second key sponsor and German brand, hansgrohe, a bathroom product specialist that had previously been involved in cyclocross, sponsoring the Superprestige series. I was reassured that this extra investment would guarantee our position rubbing shoulders with the big boys. And, of course, without hansgrohe's involvement, I would never have been photographed taking a shower for their international marketing campaign. I'm sure we'll squeeze a shot in the book somewhere for you. You're welcome.

The final major step in their development, and critical in my decision-making, was their plan to also sign up Specialized as our bike supplier on a three-year contract. Knowing that the bikes would be a consistent factor through a potentially unsettling transition was incredibly reassuring, and beyond all that, they make fucking good bikes!

And so the deal was done, and I maintain it's probably the best decision we've made in our careers. I say "we've made" because it was very much a collective decision. Like I said, I might stand on the podium from time to time, but I do so as a representative of all the guys who help get me over the line. It was as much a decision for them as for me.

And so BORA-hansgrohe has arrived in the top tier of pro cycling, and what an extraordinary start we've had. In 2017, the team, including backroom staff, has doubled while the riders have performed to an exceptional level. At one point in 2018, at the Tour de Suisse, we had the Slovakian, German, Austrian, and world road race champions all riding together. It wasn't entirely clear what the BORA-hansgrohe team jersey actually looked like!

So that's the story of my move to BORA-hansgrohe, and now we look to the future. It's such an exciting time for this vibrant young group. Funny how things work out.

WINTER

So, I mentioned that after Doha I needed to pay out on a few things. I touched on this subject earlier, but Gabriele says I need to explain exactly how this stuff works.

All joking aside, these challenges with people close to me are really important. I told you about Katarina and Lomba having to ride round Lake Tahoe, didn't I? That's what I'm talking about. With the expansion of Team Peter and the embracing of the Team Peter roster and ethos within the BORA-hansgrohe umbrella, the whole challenge thing was taking on a life of its own.

It was difficult to celebrate in Doha, but not impossible. Qatar is not a "dry" state, but it has pretty strict rules on where you can buy alcohol and where you can drink it. Anybody who has seen a Slovakian sports fan anywhere in the world will know that there is a uniform that must be carried at any time: a Slovakian flag; sports or training clothing made out of a synthetic material, usually, but not essentially, a shell suit; a branded baseball cap, preferably marketing an energy drink; and, enforceable by law in Bratislava, a maxi-size can of Pilsner Urquell lager. It is rumored that fans at the Doha world's had to obtain special permission from Slovakian diplomatic services to walk the streets of Qatar's capital without the requisite can. We are a law-abiding yet resolute country, and we stayed legal without being swayed from our destiny: to party.

When we got home, I got my little black book out and totted up who owed what.

Now, I should explain that these little side issues are not bets in the traditional sense. A bet would be "If you win, I'll do this, but if you lose, you have to do this." It's more communal than that, usually a challenge that means we all have to do something funny or crazy if it comes off.

Sometimes this is just a fun thing to pass the day. For instance, once, after a race in Belgium, we did a hansgrohe event, and then a few of us went to this really superb restaurant in Kortrijk to eat. It was me, Juraj, Giovanni, and Gabriele. While we were eating, this guy came up to me in the middle of the meal and said, "Hi, I have this brand of shoes that I'd really like you to wear." "OK," I said, swallowing a piece of steak and putting my knife and fork down, "that's nice, but I have a shoe sponsor, so I can't really do that, but thank you anyway."

"What size are you anyway? I'll bring you some."

"Well," I said, "my brother Juraj here is a 43. And my brother from another mother here, Gabriele, is a 42." That obviously wasn't what he had in mind. There was a beat as he swallowed, glancing at the two guys he'd clearly never seen or heard of.

"Sure thing. I'll bring them to your hotel in the morning." Great, see you tomorrow. Needless to say, we're still waiting.

Anyway, we were laughing away and having fun. The next thing, we were having a bet on the bill. The furthest away on guessing the total amount had to pay. We do this fairly regularly, but we don't usually eat in restaurants as swanky as this one, and let me tell you, that Giovanni Lombardi knows how to order wine.

I may have given you the impression that Gabriele is acutely aware of the cost of things, especially when it is likely to be him paying for them. This doesn't stop him losing his shirt to me on a daily basis when it comes to PlayStation. He still maintains it's a deal he has with Giovanni to keep my morale high before races. If so, my morale is very high all the time, even in the middle of winter. The challenge on this day, in this restaurant, confirmed my suspicions about Gabriele: He guessed the amount of the bill to within a euro. One euro! In a fancy restaurant at a table of men with expensive tastes showing off to each other and with the confidence of those who think they probably won't have to pay. He had obviously memorized the price of every item we'd ordered and mentally counted it all up.

The pressure was on. Giovanni does all my deals and takes care of my finances, so if he lost, I'd be more concerned than if I'd lost myself. No need to worry, he was safely within the ballpark. Me? Well, when you've been involved with this lot as long as I have, you always suspect a challenge like this might be on the cards, and you stay as alert as ... well, a sprinter. You didn't really think I'd lose, did you? Oh Juraj, my sweet, sweet brother ... get your credit card out. At least you'll have a nice new pair of invisible shoes waiting for you in the morning.

Gabriele spent most of 2016 telling the planet how I was going to win a second UCI rainbow jersey in Doha. Early in the year, he said to me that if I won, he would get the Peter Sagan logo tattooed on his ankle. "OK," I said, "very nice. And what do you want from me in return?" "I don't know," he said, "something that means a lot to you that will mean a lot to me too." "How about this?" I put my hand inside my shirt and pulled out the gold chain and crucifix I have worn since I was a teenager. "Wow. You'd do that? Yeah, let's shake on it."

There is a YouTube clip of me shooting across the finish line in Doha. As ever, the first man to greet me was Gabri, leaping with delight. You can see me shouting something and pointing wildly. You might think that it was some kind of Cristiano Ronaldo–Richard Virenque celebration, but you'd be wrong. I was pointing at Gabri and shouting, "You've got one week to get that tattoo done!"

Next, I want you to picture Giovanni Lombardi. He was known as a fox when he was a rider. In 15 years as a pro, he'd been everywhere, done everything, worked for Gianluigi Stanga, Walter Godefroot, Mario Cipollini, and Bjarne Riis and never once taken shit from anyone. He is the sort of man who would look sharp in decorator's overalls. Can you imagine a less likely candidate for a PS ankle tattoo? Well, he's got one. And he's got a white Cadillac too. That's how Doha paid out.

It must have been in the wake of this that the discussion turned to Bergen. It all sounded a bit premature to me. I haven't spent a lot of time in Norway, but I've seen enough of it to know that the roads tend to go up. And if the heat had suited me in Qatar, how the hell was I going to cope with Norway in autumn? Of course, I'd be going—I was the world champion—but it seemed a long way off. I could already feel the crosshairs resting on my shoulders as all the other candidates took aim. A hundred riders, a hundred stories, ninety-nine snipers' rifles lining me up.

That didn't stop the bets from rolling in.

At a family get-together, Dad told Lomba that he would give up smoking if I won in Norway. That was 50-odd years of dedicated puffing that he was willing to turn his back on. That was a massive motivator for me. We all think we're immortal when we're young, and teenagers growing up in Soviet Europe were no less susceptible to the lure of the cigarette than the rest of the world. We think of our parents' health as they get older, and if Dad packed in smoking, that would be a fabulous win.

Lomba had a more peculiar tobacco weakness. Somewhere along the line—I think he said it was in Sweden or somewhere in Scandinavia—he got into chewing tobacco. Nasty stuff. Dad got him to promise that he'd bin the spittoon fodder if he was going to give up cigarettes himself. Giovanni wasn't too bothered at that stage, thinking that Bergen was a long way off and a bit hilly for the more statuesque rider like the annoying Slovakian lad he kept getting stuck with.

We set some targets for 2017. We'd start in Australia at the Tour Down Under. The cycling press were talking about what a massive step up it was for BORA-hansgrohe, and why was I going to a little team like that when I could have gone to Quick-Step, Sky, or the like. They weren't seeing the bigger picture. For me, it wasn't a step up at all; it was a honing and a distillation of what we needed to achieve. No need to support a bigger team's conflicting aims. No question of a learning curve: We were a band of brothers who had done this more than once but in other jerseys, in other cars, on other massage tables, in other training plans, on different work stands. And we still had Specialized bikes to ride.

After that, the program had an asterisk planted next to the following races to signify a concerted focus:

> Flanders
>
> Roubaix
>
> California
>
> Tour
>
> Canada
>
> Bergen

OK, it was a longer list than most team leaders would target, but I liked that. If you put all your eggs in one basket and you drop it ... that's a big mess to clean up.

Bring it.

SPRING

Milan–San Remo is a cool race. I came second there in 2013 in a sprint from a little group when Fabian Cancellara and I concentrated on each other too much and got caught out by that wily German sprinter Gerald Ciolek. Hang on, I hear you say, isn't MSR something crazy like 300 kilometers? And you weren't so good at the long races then, as you have made clear over many pages? Full marks for concentration. But that year, the weather was awful, and they shortened the course. Approaching the Turchino Pass, it was snowing so hard that the race was stopped, and we all got into cars and drove through the tunnel instead! It also has to be said that the first half of the reduced race wasn't as hard as it could have been, due to the fact that nobody wanted to be out there. The snow gave way to rain, and it was generally one of the days when professional cyclists really earn their coin.

Four years on, now that I was a Monument winner, I had high hopes of doing the business in San Remo. The parcours is hard enough that the majority of bunch kickers get cleared out by the finale. The little climb of the Poggio just before the finish is short enough that it can be a springboard rather than an obstacle for me on my best form. Technical descents like that of the Poggio are fun for me, and I fancied myself in a small group on the Via Roma.

The Italians are a romantic bunch, and they all went mad when I attacked on that iconic final stretch. Not so much because it was me, but that lovely UCI rainbow jersey was ticking all their boxes. The first big race of the year, Il Primavera, the biggest Italian one-day race, the world champion . . . they love that kind of thing. And, you know what, it's supposed to be entertaining. People don't watch bike races just to find out the result. If that was the case, they would just read the paper in the morning or check their phones. Fans want drama. And if you can't make the effort to give them something to shout about when you're wearing the rainbow jersey, well, frankly you shouldn't be wearing it. People often ask if I feel the pressure of the jersey. Well, I feel the jersey, it's true, but it's not pressure. It's a responsibility to entertain.

I had a little gap going over the top and flew round the hairpins through the orchards, greenhouses, and vegetable patches of the south side of the Poggio.

It felt great. I thought I would have enough. But guess what? There's that pesky Polish opponent of mine again, good old Michal Kwiato in his new Sky jersey with the rainbow collar and cuffs scooting down behind me. Ah, you're kidding, Julian Alaphilippe too? What does a man have to do to win this race? Outsprint them, I guess.

If I'd won that sprint, I'd be telling you it was the greatest sprint in the history of cycling, but I didn't. However . . . it was a pretty damn good sprint.

I had to lead it out, unfortunately. We'd been sharing the work between the three of us as the whole race was right on top of us. I probably did a bit too much though, and when we got into town and I expected one of the others to come through, they were wedged in preparing for the sprint. I kicked hard from the front before Kwiato or Alaphilippe could jump me, and I got a gap, but the finish line was way off, and I could feel them gaining . . . we hit the line with such synchronicity that a pistol crack wouldn't have split the three of us. Kwiato and I actually hit each other as we threw our bikes at the line, but we all kept our balance. The commentators didn't know who won, but I did: Kwiato. He had judged it brilliantly. Fair play to my longest-standing rival.

Maybe I'd rather lose a fantastic bike race than win a boring one. Maybe. I don't know, but that sure was a fantastic bike race.

———

To Belgium as reigning Flanders champion as well as world champion. This was to be another great story of a day.

It was warm and dry again with the spring's first swallows swooping low across the Flemish grass and the perennial scent of chicken manure in the nostrils. Somebody told me the other day that Belgium produces so much manure that it is the only country in the world that has to export it. Is that true? Hell, I don't know, I'm a cyclist, not an agro-economist. Good fact, though, even if it's nonsense. When you come down the Koppenberg, there is a left-hander at the bottom that tightens just when you think you're around it, and beyond that bend is the biggest heap of manure in Belgium. Surely, at the rate the race comes down the hill, somebody has gone head first into it. Perhaps during the sportive the day before the race? Twenty thousand weekend warriors trying to beat their mates down the hill? All you'd see of those guys would be their shoe plates sticking out of the muck. Future archaeologists will be baffled.

Another guy who understands the meaning of entertainment is Philippe Gilbert. He's a Belgian, but not Flandrian; he's a Walloon from the other end of the country, but people love him everywhere because of the way he races. He had a year in the world champion's jersey too, so he understands that urge to please. For the past few years he's been able to wear the very cool tricolor Belgian champion's kit as well, which is probably the second-best-looking cycling kit in the world. He was at Quick-Step after many years at BMC, and they had a supremely powerful lineup for the northern classics. Like Fabian Cancellara a year before, Gilbert's supposed team leader Tom Boonen was bowing out. If he could take this, his last Flanders, it would give him four victories in the race, which would sit very neatly alongside his four Paris–Roubaix winner's cobbles. Sometimes you just have to shake your head and applaud.

Those two animated the race early on, Boonen flying up the Muur and turning the years back gloriously. In 2006, Tom won this race in the world champion's jersey, the last man to do that before me. Imagine the crowd that day! The best Flandrian winning their favorite race in the rainbow stripes. That must have been some day to be a cycling fan.

The Muur was the launchpad for many of his and other great wins back in the day, but it lost its place in the race when the finish was moved to Oudenaarde a few years back, much to the anger of the fans. It was back, though now with 90 kilometers to go instead of the old 20. Nevertheless, this was the point he picked to split the race, and split it he did. When we got to the Oude Kwaremont for the second of our three ascents, it was Gilbert's time to lay down some power. The rest of us were spread out behind as he went on a solo break with 55 kilometers of hard hills and cobbles to go. Boonen gleefully sat watching me,

Greg Van Avermaet, Kristoff, and all the others, knowing that if we hauled Gilbert back, it would be his turn to go. Quick-Step seemed as if they had all the answers. The next turning point in a day full of them was the Taaienberg. I knew that I was going to have to get rid of some people and drop the hammer from farther out if I was going to catch Gilbert and have a chance of retaining the title of De Ronde winner. Waiting wasn't an option. The Taaienberg is as good a place to start as any, a cobbled berg that would be the star of any race that didn't feature the Muur, Kwaremont, Koppenberg, or Paterberg. Tom's bid that had been shaping up so sweetly flew out the window like a rapidly deflating balloon when his chain jammed into the space between his chainset and frame, as he tried to drop it into the smaller chainring at the bottom of the climb. With the roads narrow and the race fast, quick service was impossible, and his race ended in anticlimactic disappointment.

I didn't know he was screwed; I was just going up as hard as I could, hoping I'd dropped him. Over the top, I had split the bunch down, and the remaining guys worked with me to chase Gilbert. At the top of the Kwaremont for the final time, there were 17 kilometers left and less than a minute separating Gilbert from me, GVA, and Oliver Naesen. We powered on to the long, draggy cobbled section, knowing it was all or nothing now. It was dry and dusty, and instead of my usual plan of heading down the crest of the cobbles, I went for the hard, dried-out muddy section in the left-hand gutter for maximum speed. This was the race, then and there, and I was mashing a big gear for all I was worth.

In a split second, the world turned upside down.

I think I've talked about crashes happening in slow motion sometimes. You see it coming, and everything goes into Matrix speed. Not this time. One second, I'm thinking about whether we can catch Gilbert by the top of the Paterberg, the next I'm looking at the pale blue Flemish sky like an April fool. Greg hammered into me, Naesen into him, and we all rolled across the cobbles. Greg was able to remount, but Naesen and I needed bikes. On the Kwaremont, of all places, no wider than some baths I've been in, and our team cars way behind the disintegrating bunch.

Help was on hand in the shape of the Shimano neutral service car. It shrieked to a halt in a cloud of dust, a mechanic was out in a flash plucking a bike off the roof, and Naesen was on it and gone. Before I knew what was happening, the guy was back in his car and gone. Huh? What happened? Do you see me here, buddy? Maybe he thought I was just some guy in a stripy shirt trying to help Naesen back onto his bike.

Shaking my head in stunned disbelief, I reached down into the dust to pick up my 100% sunglasses. God, I love those shades. I've never worn a rainbow jersey without them. They go together like dumplings and cheese for me (seriously, if you're ever in Slovakia you must try our national dish, bryndzové halušky). As I reached out, there was a whirring of gears and Niki Terpstra rode straight over them. Brilliant. It was that kind of day. What fresh hell awaited next? If I'd fallen into a bucket of tits that day, I'd have come out sucking my thumb.

So, I know you want to ask, would we have caught Gilbert? Would I have won? Despite the crash, Greg was only 30 seconds back on the line. You'd have outsprinted him, wouldn't you, Peter? It's immaterial. Philippe Gilbert won the race. He was easing down when he knew it was won. He might have had something left in the tank if we'd closed on him. Greg and I might have refused to help each other chase. Greg might have outsprinted me—after all, Kwiato had done it a fortnight earlier. Tom might not have jammed his frame. Cancellara might not have retired a year before. Rik Van Looy might have found a time machine. I know I'm being flippant, but there is just no end of "what ifs?" in bike racing. That's why we love it. What if I'd trained a bit harder? What if I looked where I was going? Sorry, but it's bullshit. Philippe Gilbert won a brilliant Tour of Flanders with an incredible solo break. Guess what? There were a hundred more of us with a hundred stories, but his was the only one worth telling.

210

What had caused me to fall? Well, first and foremost, my inattentiveness and poor choice of line had caused it. Next, I was fairly sure I'd caught something on the barriers. Gabriele watched it a dozen times, and he didn't think so. Most people seemed to think that I'd clipped the foot of one of the crowd barriers lining the course. I couldn't understand that, as I'd been looking down and watching the barriers, I'd been looking at one of those feet as I fell. It was fast, but I felt my bars had clipped something. Then Gabriele got sent a video from the phone of a spectator who was watching from the other side of the road. There it was, clear as day. Being warm, a spectator had removed his jacket and draped it over the barriers. That in itself probably wouldn't have stopped me, but then, of course everybody was leaning on those barriers to get a better view and unconsciously leaning on that jacket, pinning it in place. My left-hand brake lever caught the jacket. It didn't move, which yanked my bars sharply left, and then my front wheel hit the foot of the barrier.

Bizarrely, this guy with the jacket turned out to be a teacher from Holland and was a distant acquaintance of Body! When we found this out, some time had passed, and I thought it was funnier than if I'd found out there and then. Not for one moment did I blame the guy; I should have been well clear of where he was standing. I had this funny idea that we could swap my tattered and filthy rainbow jersey for his old jacket, and I could keep his jacket as a souvenir of a memorable day. He'd certainly have something in return and a story to dine out on for years to come.

Gabri talked to him on the phone. Would he like to come to Paris–Roubaix next week as a guest of BORA-hansgrohe? Do a little presentation for the press where we swap the jacket and the jersey, watch the race with us, and join us at the finish?

He said he could, but there was the cost of his travel from the Netherlands. And that jacket wasn't cheap. If we paid him his expenses and the cost of replacing the jacket, he'd check his diary. Gabriele decided against it.

The press all wanted to know the same thing. I'd been run out of the first two Monuments. Was I going to win Paris–Roubaix? I don't think like that. A hundred stories. I race, I try to win. There are just far too many variables in races like these to predict how they will pan out. I'd won races where other people were stronger than me, and I'd lost races to people whom I'd expected to beat. Everybody wants to win. Most of us will go home disappointed.

I certainly went home disappointed from Roubaix.

I found myself in my most-preferred situation. I had forced a split with my teammate Maciej Bodnar, and we had two other great engines with us, Daniel Oss and Jasper Stuyven. Just as he'd been the week before, Greg Van Avermaet was really strong, but he wouldn't chase us because his teammate Oss was in our move and was a genuine threat. (I'm pleased that Daniel has joined BORA-hansgrohe now. The man is a thoroughbred racehorse and an ox rolled into one.) In that group, even if Daniel sat on and refused to work to improve Greg's chances of catching us, there were three of us to pull, and the other teams would find it difficult to close the gap, especially on the pavé. Body was pulling like a Trojan, and the race formed and reformed countless times with the damage we were doing. Then bang! A flat. Body waited with me, I got a wheel, chased back on, and still we were at the head of the main group, with just Oss and Stuyven ahead.

On the long, hard stretch of cobbles at Mons-en-Pévèle about 60 kilometers out from the velodrome, I put my head down and smashed it as hard as I could. It's always better to be on the front on the pavé. You can pick your line, there is less dust in your face, you aren't at risk from other people's mistakes, and you're in a position to dictate the race. Oss and Stuyven were caught, and the race splintered into twos and threes for a while. Greg was with me and felt really strong. I pictured the two of us splintering the race between us in the closing stages and thought that we could whittle the list of contenders down a bit more. Štybar was at the front, and I managed to bridge across to his group alone on the Templeuve section. Just saying these place names conjures up the dust, the flat scenery, those French road signs, the banners announcing each *secteur*. This is the time when the race is won or lost, I told myself. Greg was in the group behind, as was Tom Boonen, making his bid for a record-breaking fifth Roubaix cobblestone trophy in his final race. The front group was tiring; it was the perfect time to drive home my advantage and go it alone, with the pivotal Carrefour de l'Arbre section still to come. As we hit the next section of cobbles, I drove at 99 percent to try and split it . . . and punctured.

Greg passed me as I waited for a wheel. He caught Štybar's group and went on to win alone. Chapeau, sir . . . you are a survivor and a performer, and cycling needs more like you. Personally, you could make my life easier by not beating me so often, but you are undoubtedly one of the good guys.

Twice I got away with attacks. Twice I punctured and was caught. It's been the story of Roubaix for me over the years: Ride hard, get flats at bad times.

My first DS at Liquigas, Stefano Zanatta, had always held the belief that I'd never win Paris–Roubaix. According to him, it was all a matter of technique. "Some riders just float over the top of the cobbles without really hitting them," he said. "Boonen, Museeuw, Tchmil. Peter? He just hits them too hard. He'll always puncture."

I agreed with him in some ways. Punctures aren't much to do with luck, they're a lot more to do with technique, as yours truly has proven at the Olympics. But if I hadn't thought I could win there, I'd have stopped trying. I'd take a week off, go to Amstel Gold the following week, fresh, and kick ass. Or just put my feet up with Katarina and Marlon and let everybody else get their teeth kicked in for hours on end.

On Team Peter

It's really important to me to always thank my team, win or lose. I might be the final nail banged into the finish line, but there are an awful lot of hammers, screwdrivers, toolboxes, and trips to the hardware store before I get anywhere near the win.

It's a curious anomaly about cycling: an individual sport played by teams.

The personalities of those around you are just as important as the physical skills they bring to the party. You need to trust every teammate, mechanic, DS, coach, and soigneur, and you need to predict how an individual will react in any given situation as there probably won't be time to communicate. For instance, I don't need to ask Burghardt or Bodnar to go on the front and lift the pace of the leader's group with 30 kilometers to go in a Monument

Top left: I didn't enjoy my first Olympic experience much, so when Rio rolled around, I thought I'd get the mountain bike out instead. I mean, how hard can it be?

Bottom left: I get plenty of comments regarding my bike handling in the pro peloton, but mountain biking demands a ridiculous level of skill. It's a lot of fun, though.

Top right: The best thing about doing the Rio Olympics was the opportunity to beat Gabriele at FIFA dozens of times every day. He doesn't look bitter though, does he?

Bottom right: People say that you're unlucky if you suffer two punctures in a race. I say you should be better at riding your bike.

Top left: Signing in to start the longest, hottest race anyone can remember: the 2016 UCI World Championship Road Race in Doha. I'd enjoyed my year in the rainbow jersey and I had no intention of giving it to somebody else.

Top right: Just because you expect a race to end in a sprint, it doesn't follow that it will be straightforward. Hours of predictably dull racing exploded in a battle of sprinting royalty.

Middle: The Sagan brothers celebrate their second consecutive UCI World Championship. That still sounds funny enough to bring a smile to my face.

Bottom: A podium of three former world champions is impressive at any race.

Top, left to right: The philosophy of Willi Bruckbauer and Ralph Denk has made my move to BORA-hansgrohe one of the best decisions of my career. And don't I make you want a hansgrohe shower?

Right: Milan–San Remo 2017. The best race I've ever lost. You could have thrown a blanket over Michal Kwiatkowski, Julian Alaphlippe, and me on the line.

Bottom left: The great form I'd taken into the 2017 classics was negated when I failed to notice a spectator's jacket draped over the barriers. Greg Van Avermaet and Oliver Naesen hit the pavé with me.

Bottom right: A week later and Paris–Roubaix evaded me as well. Surely I'd get a decent run at it one day?

Top: Juraj and me, riding together as pros in China in 2011. We didn't think it could get better than that. But now we're the UCI World Championship brothers.

Middle left: I'm sure there have been professional cycling teams that have enjoyed themselves more than BORA-hansgrohe. I just don't seem to be able to think of any at the moment.

Bottom left: If I hadn't had Maroš looking after me for my entire career—and I do mean my entire career—I wouldn't have won the races that I've won. It's just a fact.

Middle right: The Last Gregario, Sylwester Szmyd was the greatest climbing domestique of his generation, a fact recognized by his peers and employers, if not the history books.

Bottom right: Patxi Vila is the archetypal new generation director sportif: one of us, fitter than most riders, and happier riding his bike than driving the car.

Top left: Proof that Giovanni was a bit tasty himself in his day. Wouldn't you want a manager who was both the toughest negotiator in the business and the smartest rider in the bunch?

Bottom left: Gabriele and I with some ink. He hasn't just got my back. He's also got my face on his leg.

Top right: These guys. Giovanni and Gabriele. You'll have to go through them to get to me. Brothers.

Middle right: Gabriele is quite photogenic with a raincoat on and the hood up.

Bottom right: There is an unhealthy number of Peter Sagan logo tattoos on the ankles of folks in this photo. But we like that. It means something to us. We are Team Peter.

Top: At BORA-hansgrohe, we like to bring the party to the race. Other teams make us park farthest away at race starts because our bus is so loud.

Middle: I'd like to claim that I clipped out of my pedal for the purposes of entertainment at this sprint at the 2017 Tour. In fact, I totally messed it up, but still managed to hang on for the win.

Bottom: At the finish line, after Mark Cavendish came down horribly in that infamous sprint at Vittel in the 2017 Tour, Gabri predicted I would be in trouble. I told him he knew nothing about cycling.

Top: Watching a playback of the incident moments later: "Ok, Gabri. Maybe you do know something about cycling."

Middle top: Cav was out injured. I was out in disgrace. It happened and I moved on.

Middle bottom: Sometimes the greatest things come from our darkest moments. Within days I was on board the *Christina O* with all the most important people in my life.

Bottom left: Living it up with Gabriele and Giovanni.

Bottom right: And a world exclusive—I slipped on deck and smashed my teeth in. Everyone was sworn to secrecy, but I'm coming clean!

Top: The UCI rainbow jersey goes over the cobbles of the Hell of the North.

Middle: Moments like winning on the old velodrome at Roubaix will never be forgotten. This is why I do it. Training in the rain and snow. It's no price to pay at all. This is priceless.

Bottom left: And when the people who mean the most to you are the people that put you there, the celebrations are all the more poignant.

Bottom right: I got my cobble after all.

if we're all still there. They know that's the best way to keep the race together, and they've got the ability to do it.

Since I was very young, I've come to trust and rely on a select bunch of guys that are as crucial to getting results as, I don't know, training or having a bike that works. Thanks to the patience and willingness of Willi and Ralph at BORA-hansgrohe, we're all together under the same banner, and long may it continue. With Willi and Ralph, it's not a case of negotiation, they don't just allow the presence of Team Peter guys within the setup to indulge me; they recognize the worth that each and every individual brings to the whole operation.

Teammates aren't really what I mean when I talk about Team Peter. It's a team within a team, and as lucky as I am to have had the likes of Marcus Burghardt, Maciej Bodnar, and Daniel Oss at my side at varying times throughout my career, they're professional cyclists who will always bury themselves for their leader. Yes, OK, we're good friends, but when Daniel was at BMC, he rightly gave Greg Van Avermaet every last drop of sweat, just as he did for me at Cannondale and now does for me again at BORA-hansgrohe.

The point of Team Peter is that it's a little hard-core group of dedicated people whose joint goal is to make wins for me. And that's why thanking them is so important. They'll often have sacrificed personal goals and ambitions for the good of Team Peter, and when I'm on a podium, it may sound cheesy, but I really am taking a bow for all of us.

The original member of Team Peter was there long before anybody conceived the idea. In fact, he was there before I was conceived. Take a bow, Juraj Sagan. Being the middle brother is never going to be easy, and when your kid brother, totally spoiled by every member of the family, turns out to be a loud-mouth who's good at cycling, that's not going to help. Especially when you're the prominent cycling fan. I can remember coming into the house on long, hot school holiday afternoons to see Juraj crouched in front of the TV, excitedly telling me, "Pantani's put two minutes into Ullrich on Plateau de Beille!" to which I'd go, "Whatever," and shoot out the door with a rope ladder and a catapult. Pantani was the bald one. That was as far as it went for me. It was Juraj who took our races seriously, laying out his kit the night before, cleaning his chain, polishing his shoes, and talking through strategy, while I'd turn up in plimsolls on our sister's bike and attack from the start. I must have been rather irritating, but he was only ever proud of me. And then we've been able to ride together our whole professional careers! How many brothers can say something as cool as that? I can't begin to tell you what it means to win the UCI World Championship and be able to celebrate on the line with somebody else who truly understands what it means to a Sagan or a Slovakian, and somebody who has done more than anybody to help you reach that goal. It's special.

Of course, Juraj has been our national champion in his own right too. The best thing about Juraj as a cyclist, beyond his dedication and loyalty, which go without saying, is that at the age of 29 he is demonstrably improving. He's there in the closing stages at the big races and riding with a confidence and authority that puts a huge extra weapon in the arsenal for BORA-hansgrohe.

The other great advantage for me in having Juraj around is that he is so hilariously, impossibly, illogically unlucky when it comes to all the stupid daily bets and challenges we foist upon each other. If Team Peter is going out for a meal, I basically don't want to go unless Juraj is going. My chances of having to pick up the tab are halved the second he walks through the door.

Now, let me tell you about the captain of Team Peter and the man who first planted the seed and nurtured it into the self-supporting behemoth it is today. He's a bit of a behemoth himself. Of course I'm talking about the greatest agent in cycling, Giovanni Lombardi. When I was first introduced to Lomba, I was a new professional at Liquigas, and he wasn't long packed up as a rider. He had started out as a very rapid and smooth sprinter, with a nice set of Giro d'Italia stage victories to his name, but it wasn't long before his greatest skill was brought to bear on his cycling career: his nose for the best course of action. This man always knows the right path. If I find myself with a problem, I'll always ask myself: "What would Lomba do?"

In terms of his own cycling career, while he was pretty swift, he wasn't Mario Cipollini. So he went to the team with the second best sprinter, Erik Zabel, and said, "I can help you beat Cipollini." Five of Zabel's six Tour de France green jerseys came during Lomba's tenure with the team, where he built himself a reputation as the lead-out man's lead-out man. He went on to do a similar job for Cipo himself as the Lion King basked in the glorious Indian summer of his career.

He'd always had a reputation for being good at handling statistics in the bunch. In the mountains on a grand tour, Giovanni would always know what speed the bunch needed to ride at to avoid elimination. He got it down to a fine art, the autobus of flatlanders coasting home after a relaxed day with a minute or so to spare on the clock. That trust thing was in evidence right back then. His head for numbers made him a good candidate to become a riders' agent when he retired, with his knowledge of life on the other side of the barriers a huge asset. But as handy as his calculator brain is, it is certainly not the key skill that makes Giovanni the king of his chosen profession. That is the absolute refusal to deal with any problem—and they are legion and diverse—with anything other than a direct head-on approach. What is the problem? How do we fix it? Simple questions, but sometimes very difficult to ask. I am certain that if I ever sit down at a negotiating table and Giovanni is on the other side, not only will I lose, but also my life must have taken an inexplicable, unplanned, and horrific turn for the worse. He shows no fear, and he knows what everybody else around the table wants to achieve, but also the bare minimum they can live with. He makes it happen.

At Tinkoff, I remember the night before the Tour de France began in Utrecht in 2015, Oleg wanted to meet me to talk about money and bonuses and all that sort of Oleg stuff, so I wisely took Giovanni with me. We got there before Oleg, but Stefano Feltrin, who was his general manager then, was there. It's fair to say Team Peter used to rub up against Feltrin on a fairly regular basis. Not only did he control the purse strings, he also resented agreeing to what he saw as our constant and unreasonable demands. I thought we'd just wait for Oleg, but this was just too good an opportunity for Lomba to miss.

"Are you sleeping OK, Stefano?" Giovanni said.

"Yes," he replied warily, "why do you ask?"

"I suppose I just assume you sit up all night figuring out ingenious new ways to fuck riders over. To save a few euros for Oleg so you can wedge your tongue even farther up his asshole."

Stefano picked up his mobile phone and hurled it against the wall, where it splintered into a million pieces that Steve

Jobs would have struggled to identify. Who knows, maybe they are all still under a corner of carpet in that anonymous Dutch hotel room.

Feltrin was irate. He looked like a Looney Tunes character with steam rising from his ears accompanied by klaxons and heat warnings.

"Giovanni, let me tell you something. If you have to ask me if I'm fucking you, then I'm not fucking you. Because when I fuck you in the ass, it's going to be the worst ass-fucking you've ever had, and you won't be in any doubt what's happening. You'll recognize it. God knows you've had more than your fair share of ass-fucking."

Giovanni smiled and treated him to a little laugh, then Oleg walked in, and it was never mentioned again.

I believe Lomba is still waiting for the ass-fucking.

The next longest serving member of Team Peter is Maroš Hlad. He may not be the first masseur to ever give my legs a polish, but I remember getting a massage from Maroš when I was a teenager back in Žilina and thinking that I must have made it as a cyclist. This bloke was incredible. Did you ever make a deal with yourself as a kid along the lines of: "When I'm rich, I'll . . . wear new socks every day. Buy my mum a new car. Only ever use the expensive gas for my car." Something like that? Mine was: "When I've made it, I'll get a massage from Maroš every day."

And, thanks to my teams and Giovanni's exemplary negotiating skills, I do. He comes everywhere with me.

That trust and belief in the people around you couldn't be better illustrated than my relationship with Maroš. He's such a calming, even-tempered presence in my life. I don't think I've ever had a massage and not come out of the room in a better mood than when I went in. What's that poem? If you can meet with triumph and disaster and treat those two imposters just the same? That's Maroš. He's happy but restrained when we win and calm and philosophical when we lose. It goes without saying that he's an excellent masseur, but his intimate knowledge of my bizarrely twisted and knackered body is obviously something that it would take years for any other physio to sort out, no matter how skillful they are. I can't imagine life without the guy. In Brazil for the Olympics, we rented a house on the beach, just Giovanni, Gabriele, Maroš, and me, chewing the fat every night as the sun sank into the Atlantic. I've rarely been happier.

I don't know if I've become more difficult to massage over the years or whether I've just become more demanding, but at some point, I just had too much leg for Maroš to manage on his own, so he called for help. So now both Maroš and I are grateful to have Peter Kalany on our side. This is probably the most accurate representation of the phrase "I could do with an extra pair of hands" to ever be set down on paper. If I shut my eyes, could I tell which one of them was working on me? Come on, don't ask me that.

One of the hardest things about being a professional cyclist is renegotiating your contract each year when you've spent the previous 12 months burying yourself and your own chances of getting a favorable result. Come September, the team manager looks at your results and says, "Yeeeeaaah. Not much on here is there?" It's so ridiculously unfair. Everybody knows it's unfair, everybody complains about it, and then they perpetuate it, year in, year out. The guy who spent the summer hiding but got into a break on one of those lazy, steamy, dog-days in July when the Tour de France raises a truce flag picks up a barrel of UCI points for outsprinting a 40-year-old in Montpellier or Carpentras and sticks a zero on his contract for next year. Meanwhile, his teammate who spent three weeks keeping his G.C. contender-leader out of the wind, pacing him up the Ventoux and the Tourmalet, trotting back to the car for water every half an hour, giving up his bike when the star's gears pack up, and then crawls into bed exhausted each night is out on his ear because he earned no points.

This is all a lead-up to me telling you that you shouldn't worry if you haven't heard of a Polish cyclist called Sylwester Szmyd. If I was to tell you that he was a professional for top teams for fully 17 years without winning anything other than a stage of the Dauphiné once, you might think I'm damning him with faint praise or paying him a backhanded compliment, but nothing could be further from the truth. Just stop to imagine for a moment how good a domestique you would have to be to so completely subsume your own podium dreams in support of your team that you barely ever threaten to win a race, yet your name is inked onto the team sheet race after race, month after month, season after season for the likes of Liquigas, Lampre, and Movistar as an absolute prerequisite for the team's success. Reliable climbing domestiques are like hen's teeth, and good teams know when they find one. Alejandro Valverde and Nairo Quintana knew a man they could rely upon when they saw him.

Sylwester was at Liquigas when I turned pro, and I thought he was just the best. He never complained, he never questioned, he just did it, day in, day out, every day. And boy, could he climb. He made it look easy, his skinny legs and Polish complexion making him look like a ribbon of pasta on a bike as he disappeared up the road in front of you.

Plus, he had the coolest nickname in cycling. When he was a young professional, he rode in the service of the legendary Marco Pantani at Mercatone Uno, shepherding arguably the greatest climber the sport has ever seen over the mountain passes of Europe. As the years went on, Sylwester kept putting his signature on new contracts, and his old teammates kept retiring. Pantani himself was dead in a tragic derailment of his own story. One day, somebody, one of his old Italian teammates on his own retirement, said, "Hey, Sylwester, you're the last one of us left. The last of Pantani's teammates still riding. You're the Last Gregario."

The Last Gregario. That's a movie anybody would pay to see.

And now, having been a neighbor, mentor, and training partner for many years, Sylwester has finally retired and is officially my personal coach. No smoking cigarettes behind the wheel of a team car for The Last Gregario though . . . he hates it when he can't ride with us, and you can see him itching when the races start without him.

Oh yeah, and that single stage he won? It finished on top of Mont Ventoux. If you're only going to do something once, do it properly, eh?

The most cerebrally gifted member of Team Peter has got quite a story of his own. Patxi Vila comes from that never-ending production line of classy Basque riders raised on the slopes of the Jaizkibel, Euskadi's holy cycling mountain. You're born on a bike if you're born here, and professional teams sign up infants faster than you can say *vamos*! But Patxi, good as he is, didn't leap into the first offers that came his way. He was determined to study and build up some qualifications first. By the time he signed a professional contract with Banesto, he was

25, having completed his degree in sports science before taking to the road.

Even as a pro, he was determined to sample all he could of life, leading him to work daily with people living with Down syndrome. He became a classy Giro d'Italia, Tour de France, and Vuelta a España competitor, securing the unfathomable and surely unique record of finishing in a quietly excellent 22nd position in each of the three Grand Tours. Not content with arriving in the pro peloton late, he left it early too, joining Specialized as the main man charged with making their bikes the absolute best available. Now, my view on bikes isn't complicated—if it works, that's good enough for me—but knowing Patxi has given Specialized his input over the years is incredibly reassuring.

After a stint with Specialized and their S-Works factory people, Patxi took up a new role on the coaching staff at Tinkoff, where he could still work with those bikes but from the athlete's standpoint, rather than the manufacturer's. He became my coach at the time when I was at my lowest ebb and managed to turn my career—my whole life—around in a matter of weeks. He has the generosity of spirit to suggest that I have helped his career as much as he's helped mine, but the man put a hand on my shoulder and pulled me back from the edge. That's something I'll never forget, and I don't intend to let him walk away from Team Peter too easily either.

He's become the technical rock that we depend upon, directing from the saddle rather than behind the wheel wherever possible. He's our DS now, with Sylwester taking on the personal coaching role that was the start of things between Patxi and me.

Oh, and how cool is this? When you see Patxi on the morning of a big race, the conversation will often go like this:

"Hey, Patxi. How are you this morning?"

"Ready."

Come on, that's cool, right?

It's nice to have a DS that understands bikes as well as he understands riders, but there are some other guys on any team that need to really know their bikes. I'm referring of course to the mechanics. If they get it wrong, I can't win. If they get it really wrong, I might not come back in one piece. And if I'm worrying about not winning or not coming back in one piece, then my chances of success take a huge hit.

Step forward Jan Bachleda and Mindaugas Goncaras. In my opinion, these guys are the best mechanics in the business and invaluable members of Team Peter. If they told me it was safe to jump in a barrel and be tossed over the Niagara Falls, I'd hop right in. That said, I'd hope that someone important would forbid me from doing so.

So that's it for the inner workings of Team Peter. You already know all about Ján Valach—unquestionably an integral member of Team Peter—so that's all the important characters, all the different professionals and brilliant people that make my job so enjoyable and who have contributed directly to the successes we've had together.

Yep. Everyone. Cheers. Speak to you later.

What?

Oh, OK, Gabriele, don't cry, I'm only teasing you. Yes, ladies and gentlemen, Mr. Gabriele Uboldi, at my side for every minute of every day, keeping me out of trouble, letting me win at games. Take a look at photos of me on social media, and you'll no doubt spot him within seconds. The international man of mystery who comes to us from Genoa via Valencia, former professional Las Vegas poker star, America's Cup insider, and owner of more dogs than most people have underpants. Gabriele is the very living embodiment of Team Peter. As with all the others listed above, he's absolutely essential to the system, he dedicates his life to our success, spends huge parts of every day sorting out shit, is always there for me anywhere in the world whatever the time zone, yet the real reason we all end up spending so much time together is because we really like each other.

Team Peter. I'm a lucky guy and I know it.

SUMMER

It hadn't been a bad start to the year, but it hadn't been ideal. Kwiato had edged me out of San Remo with the sprint to end all sprints. My bid to add the 101st Tour of Flanders to the 100th had been clotheslined. My glasses got broken. I'd had a string of second places (again) and nearly been hit by a lady walking her dog.

To be fair, she was on a zebra crossing and I was riding on the road rather than the cycle path. The only mitigating circumstances on my behalf was that it was during the time trial of Tirreno–Adriatico in San Benedetto del Tronto. Nobody had told her.

Anyway, I thought I was due a change of luck. BORA-hansgrohe provided a perfectly relaxed professional environment, with far fewer politics to contend with and no competing interests. This isn't a criticism of how things had been at Tinkoff, just an acknowledgment that bigger teams are bound to have to deal with those kind of issues. My form was good for the summer. I'd picked up three points classifications already at Tirreno, California, and Switzerland, and had my eyes set on equaling Erik Zabel's record with a sixth straight green jersey at the Tour de France.

Once again, the race was starting outside France, this time in Düsseldorf, Germany. It meant more logistical questions and long transfers early in the race, but spare a thought for Giro d'Italia competitors. I've yet to ride it—one day—but recent years have taken the start to Scandinavia, Northern Ireland, and, in 2018, Israel! It makes good press I guess, but the general effect on riders and especially team staff is increased stress and tiredness, generally at a time when the race is at its most dangerous.

Speaking of dangerous, it poured rain for the opening time trial stage of the Tour in Germany. I'm glad I didn't consider myself as an overall contender or feel as though I could compete on the stage, as the pressure to test your limits in those conditions is huge. That's what happened to Alessandro Valverde, whose midthirties have been his golden years. He was coming into the race as dual leader of the Movistar team with Nairo Quintana, a really powerful proposition, but found himself in hospital before the day was out, having lost traction in the wet and thumped into the barriers.

The following day took us into Belgium and was affected by heavy showers again. Chris Froome went down this time but managed to regain the bunch before we began to line up for the sprint.

What is a sprint? That's right. A sprint is very often a lottery. I found myself on the front this time, rather than covered up as I would have liked, and when I opened up the throttle, Kittel, Greipel, Cavendish, et al. were already flying. I was swamped, only a couple of lengths behind Marcel Kittel on the line, but in 10th, way down on the German drag racer.

Stage 3 looked more to my liking. Finally, we would enter France, but the terrain in Lorraine looked more difficult, the race organizers having chosen a flatter route into Liège than fans of Liège–Bastogne–Liège have come to recognize. The finish comprised a short, sharp climb to the line, a type of course that had always been good to me at the Tour, right back to my first ever stage win at Seraing. That was not so far from here, either. It felt good.

The first thing on a day like that was to make sure that a break didn't stay away, always tricky on a twisty, rolling stage on smaller roads. That first hour was insane as a result, everybody trying to get into a break before the day settled down. After a very fluid day, we approached the finish *gruppo compacto*, and my chances of winning were helped by a nasty little 11 percent climb within the last 2 kilometers. That was enough to break up the sprint teams' lead-out trains and take some of the fast guys out of the equation.

The G.C. contenders were sensibly staying near the front to reduce the risk of lost seconds to each other at the tricky finish, and as we came to the bottom of the ramp up to the line, it was the likes of Alberto and Froomey around me rather than Greipel and Kittel. Richie Porte was there for the same reason but saw a glimpse of a stage win, and he took off with about 500 meters remaining. It was the ideal launchpad for me, and I went around him, my initial burst enough to put daylight between me, Greg Van Avermaet, and Michael Matthews. A comfortable win beckoned. And then I pulled my foot out of the pedal, just like at Richmond. Unbelievable.

Once again, fortunately, I didn't lose my balance or my momentum. I was able to clip back in and begin to sprint again, biting down the panic. I just had enough left to relax on the line and give a regal salute, like I'd planned the whole thing all along. You know that saying about the swan—serene on the surface while its feet paddle like mad below the water? That's how it was, but with webbed feet in bike pedals.

It's so good to win at the Tour. The whole world knows. And winning in the world champion's jersey was pretty special. I wasn't planning on wearing it for too much longer in this race, though. I fancied that green one. Stage 3 had been a good one to win regarding green, as I scored heavily with most of my rivals out of the running, and I clawed back some of the advantage they'd taken from me the day before. With another likely sprint day tomorrow, I thought I could stay competitive and see where we were come the next weekend.

I had no inkling that the seemingly straightforward, flat stage from Luxembourg to Vittel would be the most momentous of my whole Tour de France career.

Until the last 300 meters, it was indeed straightforward. A long, lovely day following the Mosel with nothing much to report, so I won't bore you with that. But I will try to give you my account of what happened at the finish line, firstly in real time as it happened for me, then with the benefit of replays.

Dimension Data started winding up the pace, then Lotto took it up for Greipel, but the man to really open the sprint was Alexander Kristoff. He likes the long, sustained outside-lane power drive over the sharp burst, and he was traveling pretty swiftly. I was trying to follow him, but was suddenly aware of the other sprinters whooshing toward me from my left. Forced right, I felt a nudge on my right as the distance between me and the barriers shrunk dramatically. I heard a yell and the unmistakable metal-on-carbon-on-Lycra-on-tarmac sound of a crash. A moment later, Arnaud Démare had won the stage, I was second and Kristoff third, but Mark Cavendish, John Degenkolb, and Ben Swift were all on the ground.

I learned it was Cav who'd gone down next to me. Shit, it sounded like a bad one, and we were certainly traveling fast. When I saw Gabriele 100 meters past the line, he was grim-faced, and I was instantly worried that somebody, probably Cav, was seriously injured. He put his arm round me and ushered me quickly toward the BORA-hansgrohe bus. "Peter," he said, "we have a problem." Huh? We have a problem? I knew that the sprint had ended badly, and people might be hurt. We take our lives in our hands every time we try to win a Tour de France stage with nothing but a poly-styrene lid and leather mitts to protect us from the road.

Cav and I had touched at high speed, and either one of us could have gone down, but he was the unlucky one. But now Gabri was telling me that we had a problem. We? Me? Why?

We watched the playback. Oh shit. As we get squeezed and Cav is on my right, you can clearly see my elbow come out into him. It looked bad.

Immediately, I said sorry to Cav. Not "Sorry I pushed you off," you understand, but, "Sorry you crashed." There is a brother-hood among sprinters: You have to respect each other's safety, and you have to feel for each other when it goes wrong. It was Cav today, but it could have easily been the other way around, and maybe tomorrow it would be.

Within minutes, the race jury announced that I had been demoted to last in the bunch, with a penalty of 30 seconds in the general classification and 80 points in the points classification. I was now out of the top 10 on G.C. and falling down the green jersey rankings.

Cav had broken his shoulder and cut his hand quite badly. He was definitely out of the race. Then, abruptly, so was I. Following a protest from Dimension Data, the Tour de France kicked me out.

It seemed that veering off my line had been enough to earn me the original punishment, but they agreed with Dimension Data that I had deliberately elbowed Mark to the floor.

It wasn't true. I didn't deliberately elbow him. We protested, but to no avail. Cav was out injured, and I was out disqualified.

I love Mark Cavendish. I am fond of saying that though we cyclists race against each other many times, we never really get to know each other unless we make friends away from racing, and very few of us do so. Mark is a little bit different because he wears his heart on his sleeve. He's so unreserved and openly emotional that he's very easy to like and understand. You feel like you know him when you've only met a few times, and by 2017 we had been together on countless occasions. That evening I called him to find out how he was. It was a really difficult time for him. He'd broken the same shoulder before, crashing at the Tour in

Yorkshire a few years ago, and it wasn't in the same position that it had once been, not to mention a bit weaker. He was very down and was clearly in two minds about the incident. He knew that I didn't bear him any personal ill will, and he knew I was worried about him, but still the idea that I had used my elbow to make him crash was hard for him to process. I thought that he had been egged on a bit by his team—his DS had made a few forthright comments—but they would no doubt claim they were trying to protect him. I know Gabri and my crew would do exactly the same if the tables were turned.

Other riders were equally damning of me. Andre Greipel said, "We're not friends anymore."

OK, so that's what happened that day. I know what I think really happened, and I think that the jury made a mistake. I've gone over it with my teammates and friends many times, read everything, watched everything, seen every angle, heard every opinion. Let's go through it, and I'll explain the whole sorry tale from my perspective. You're allowed to skip this bit if you've heard enough already. Don't worry, I hear you.

Andre Greipel is getting a nice lead-out from his last teammate when Kristoff starts that long windup to his top speed with Bouhanni on his wheel. Seeing Kristoff pass to his right, Greipel thinks, *There goes my train,* and goes for his wheel, inadvertently squeezing Bouhanni right.

Behind Bouhanni and to his right, coming from farther back at higher speed, is Arnaud Démare. He is squeezed farther right by the whole concertina effect started by Greipel. It's like flicking a piece of rope and watching the ripple pass along it. This is nobody's fault: just cycling, sprinting in particular, and the laws of physics. Bouhanni's and Démare's movements push me in the same direction, and the last man in the line is Mark Cavendish. There were five in the bed, and the little one said, "Roll over," so we all rolled over, and one fell out. What started as a sprint in the middle of the road has suddenly become a sprint up against the barriers, and Cav has been cast in the role of the unlucky man when the space runs out. We all rolled over, and one fell out.

So far so logical, but what happens next is why I ended up back in Monaco while the race headed for the Alps. On the video, as I try to keep my balance in the squeeze, my elbow suddenly juts out, and Cav goes down hard, all in one movement. This is the point where the race jury make their error. I didn't deliberately put my elbow out. In fact, I didn't put my elbow out at all, even to help keep my balance, as some have speculated. This is what happened: Mark is going faster than I, but into a gap that is rapidly disappearing. As he and I touch, his angle and extra speed mean that his left-hand brake lever hits the back of my right forearm. It's that collision that nearly causes both, or maybe all of us, to crash, but directly results in him going down onto that ill-fated right shoulder. My elbow coming out is the result of that contact, not the cause of it.

I understand that it looked bad, just as I'm sure you can understand why I was so surprised to be told I'd caused the crash. With a less histrionic reaction and a bit more professional understanding, the situation could have been much more sensibly resolved. Instead it turned quickly into a massive political mess.

Leaving aside the severity of Mark's injuries and the repercussions of me getting thrown out of the race for a moment, I would also argue that my original punishment for leaving my line was also unjust. I didn't deliberately choose to go right; I had no choice. What was I meant to do, crash? Knock everybody else off? If I was to be demoted, then all of us should be: Greipel, Bouhanni, Démare, and I had all in turn moved across the road, but in legitimate racing moves, not in dangerous or calculated "professional fouls."

The whole thing began to simmer down. Mark and I exchanged some supportive tweets and messages. Andre Greipel, being the gentleman that he is, apologized for his heat-of-the-moment reaction and told his team Lotto that they were also wrong to blame me, which he didn't have to do, and I really appreciated that.

But then, just as it seemed like we were moving on, the UCI came out with a big statement about how they were going to increase their finish-line analysis because of what Peter Sagan did in the Tour de France! Dimension Data opened it all up again by demanding a retrospective ban for me. For fuck's sake. Let it go. It's racing. It happened. I wasn't trying to kill anybody, least of all my friend Mark Cavendish. When you see some of the punching and headbutting that goes on in the melee that is a Tour stage sprint finish, all this fuss about me and him was ridiculous.

I was really hoping that Mark might go on Twitter to tell the world that it was a bit of a joke, but that was his decision to make. Not mine, and I respect that. It would also have obviously been in opposition to his team's position, which is never a good place to be. And at the end of the day, it would have further prolonged the agony and left the patient—cycling's credibility—stuck in the emergency room, waiting to be released back into a world that had long since moved on.

––––––

I wasn't the best of company for a few days. But you can't sit around feeling sorry for yourself forever.

The emotion that finally got me off my ass and into a mood of frenzied activity was the feeling that I'd let everybody down: BORA-hansgrohe and Willi for the faith and cash they'd invested in me and the huge sense of anticlimax that follows your prize possession being unable to deliver one of the main things they'd brought you along for. Giovanni, Gabriele, Maroš ... all of Team Peter for working so hard to make things like the Tour happen then having to face it not happening after all. My teammates were focused and dedicated to the Tour, each one with a clear purpose, then the pointy bit of their intercontinental ballistic missile was removed and decommissioned. But the hurt I felt most acutely was for my family and friends who saw it all unfold, powerless to intervene, who heard and read all the bad things being said about me and felt fiercely obligated to defend and protect me. You understand the true nature of "supporters" on days like those.

I needed to do something—anything—to break the mood I'd fallen into, but more specifically I wanted to do something for all those people. My teammates and friends on the team were beyond my reach with more than two weeks of the Tour remaining, but they knew I was with them in spirit and would have been there in reality but for the intervention of the race jury.

But my friends, family, and the Team Peter gang not still engaged on the race . . . I could do something for them.

Hmm. What was Monte Carlo good for? I got on the phone to the yacht brokers. Could you perhaps organize a yacht for about 10 people to have a holiday next week? You could? Great. A bit later, they called back. Yes, they could organize a yacht for 10, no problem. But if I was interested . . .

Once upon a time, the richest man in the world was a Greek shipping magnate called Aristotle Onassis. Now, shipping magnates are expected to have luxurious boats. This being after the

Second World War, the seas were awash with ships no longer being used for what their builders intended, namely sinking other boats or trying to stop other boats sinking other boats. One such vessel was HMCS *Stormont*, a Canadian frigate that had protected merchant shipping in the Battle of the Atlantic, then helped land allied troops on the Normandy beaches on D-Day. Ninety-nine meters of sleek seafaring quality would make the ideal vessel for Onassis's alchemists to create the most opulent floating palace the world had ever seen. The conversion cost him $4 million . . . that's $4 million at 1954 prices. Bearing in mind this was during the period of crushing postwar austerity, this lavish display of wealth must have put a fair few noses out of joint. Finished, she was the most desirable ship afloat and, to many, remains so today. He named her after his daughter Christina.

The *Christina O* had played host to the likes of Richard Burton and Elizabeth Taylor, Grace Kelly, and the Monégasque royal family, Frank Sinatra . . . Winston Churchill had smoked cigars on her expansive rear deck. Jackie Onassis had of course spent long hot days at sea avoiding the crowds, despite the rumors that her late husband John F. Kennedy had frolicked below decks with a certain Marilyn Monroe in his time.

Now, 20 years after a $50 million spruce-up reconfirmed her as Queen of the Med, she went out on private hire if you had the cash, and the patience to wait five years for the chance. It just so happened that they'd had a cancellation. I could hire her for my holiday, but we'd have to sail from Monte Carlo tomorrow.

OK, I'll take it.

The rest of the day was a blur. I had to get the message to everybody that they had to be in Monaco tomorrow, and then I had to book and pay for flights for everyone. It was a whirl of Internet, travel agents, constantly ringing phones, numerous call backs, credit card pummeling, passport numbers, and connecting flights. Normally this would be the sort of thing Gabri would do for me, but I hadn't done my job during the Tour, so it was time for me to do his job and make it up to him.

I could scarcely believe it when we set sail into the gorgeous, azure July Mediterranean the next day with 28 of us on board.

It is an unfortunate fact that, still in my twenties, I am condemned for the rest of my life to never have a better holiday than those mystical, magical days aboard *Christina O*. The sun resolutely refused to stop shining until it was forced, complaining over the horizon each night by beautiful cool night skies. Sea birds and schools of glittering fishes trailed us like court followers of Louis XIV. We cruised along the Riviera and the Ligurian coast, taking in the sights in a way that isn't really possible when you're flying up the Cipressa or the Poggio as I have been when previously passing through San Remo and the rest of this coast. You see a lot of lovely places on bike races, but I can rarely remember being as enchanted by anywhere as crazily beautiful as Portofino where all of us spent a glorious afternoon meandering through the shady narrow streets between tall, colorful houses or dangling our feet between shivering shoals of silver fishes in the shallows.

We ate like those indulged favorites of the Sun King. We drank like prohibition started in a week's time, which for me, back on the bike, it would. Gabriele leapt from the deck into the cool blue waters, showing off his new tattoo. It was a fantastic portrait of Heath Ledger's Joker in *The Dark Knight*, accompanied by the immortal line: "Why so serious?" Where did he get an idea like that?

Time spent with the people you love most is never time wasted, even if you just spend it wasting time. It's beautiful.

The boat itself. I don't know where to start. Hell, no, I know where to start: at the rear deck. This huge, open area was dominated by a beautiful swimming pool, the bottom of which was covered in the most captivating mosaic of Theseus and the Minotaur doing battle. Many a happy hour was wasted here in the heat of the day. Then, as night began to settle around us, a switch would be flicked, the pool would drain away, and the bottom would rise until flush with the rest of the deck, and we had ourselves a Minotaur-themed dance floor on which to party until the sun came back.

I was talking to the skipper—I hope you didn't think I was piloting this thing myself—about the opulence, and he claimed that the seats were covered in a special kind of leather made from whales' foreskins. It sounds unlikely, I know, but until I see lab results showing the contrary, I'm sticking with it.

I just let life happen for a few days. It was so refreshing to not find myself trying to control everything all the time. There are some things you can't control, like the weather, like a flick of direction in a sprint, or somebody else's perception of your elbow movements.

I couldn't control the UCI, ASO, or the race jury, but I could control my own condition and my actions, and that was what I would do from this point forward.

One more thing I clearly couldn't control was my balance. I slipped approaching the onboard jacuzzi and went headlong into the far side, face first, knocking out my two front teeth. These teeth, the teeth that replaced my milk teeth at nine years old, had served me well up to that point, surviving all the crashes that have happened to me in cycling. We resolved not to tell anyone lest we—well, just me—got into trouble and *Christina O* got the blame. I had already begun to realize that she was the key to everything. There was no glorious end to the season, no Bergen, no shot at a third consecutive world's without *Christina O*. My floating palace of redemption.

Ah well, I can't control everything, as we have established, but I can find a dentist.

On the Other Guys

People often ask me about other cyclists. "Hey, Peto, what's Kristoff like? Froomey? Spartacus?"

The truth is that I don't really know. Obviously, I know them, and we're very rarely anything other than courteous, respectful, and caring toward each other, but *know them*? Not really. Likewise, they might be able to tell you things about how I ride a bike, how I'm likely to react in certain circumstances, maybe a story or anecdote, but none of those guys could say they really know me.

People say that we work together, but that's not really true. Let's say you have a shop in the high street. A butcher's. Now, you're going to get to know the guys in your shop better, obviously. So if your butcher's is successful and everybody likes working there, over a few years you're going to get to know people like Maciej Bodnar, Roman Kreuziger, and Marcus Burghardt.

But how about that guy Tom who works at the bakery down the street? Seems a nice fellow. We had a chat over a beer at the Christmas party last year. Dumoulin, I think his surname is. And what about that guy in the hairdresser's? Dashing chap . . . Marcel maybe? Yeah, decent guy. You see my point. You don't actually work together, and the fleeting nature of professional cycling means that by the time you get to know somebody, they've moved on.

And then of course we're doing different jobs that don't interweave as much as you may think. I saw Alberto at maybe two races in 2015 because we had very different schedules, even though we were teammates. Some teams—Sky does it like this—break their weighty squads down into units like the classics unit, the Giro unit, and the Spanish unit, with the same riders, masseurs, mechanics, coaches, and DSs working together throughout the year, and they'll only cross-pollinate when something changes. We're lucky at BORA-hansgrohe because we're not so big that we don't all know each other, though we may have to do something like that as we grow, and it's already harder for new guys coming in at the start of the season.

I've got some good pro cycling pals that I see out of the race environment for a beer or a pizza, but they tend to be guys that you choose to live near or train with, like Sylwester Szmyd, who's been a friend, training partner, and neighbor for years and is my coach now. Oscar Gatto is one of the few who I hang out with but don't share an employer with.

All I can tell you about the other guys in the peloton is how I find them to ride with or against. There is virtually nobody I can think of whom I don't get along with, at least on the superficial basis of people who share a workspace. Even Mark Cavendish, with whom I've inadvertently created one of the most-reported controversies of the 2017 season, would say there's a mutual respect between us. I certainly would. We're a bunch of guys who compete fiercely at an elite level in a sport where the difference between success and failure can boil down to the click of a camera shutter.

The different schedules we all have each season also mean that I have not spent a great deal of my life chatting with many of the biggest names in our sport. For example, I hardly know Alejandro Valverde and Nairo Quintana, giants of the game as twin leaders of Movistar. We have never got beyond amiable smiles and hellos, because our paths just don't really cross. Sylwester rode with them both for years, and he says the dynamic is very interesting, with Valverde's years of experience making him the skipper, but Quintana's reputation outside of the team, especially in South America, is immense, giving them a relationship not unlike the captain of the flagship and the admiral of the fleet. Listen to me, straight into the gossip, and this is just the stuff that Sylwester told me, I haven't got a clue. When Sylwester and his wife went on honeymoon to Colombia, it turned out that Quintana had quietly and personally organized every last detail to make sure they had the best possible holiday. He's that type of guy.

Chris Froome is always very friendly and a model of dedication, not just to the sport but also in the loyalty he shows his team. The rest of the world might speculate about his standing in the sport, but he just keeps his head down and continues to perform. Talking to Gabriele and Giovanni over dinner, the consensus is that it's scarcely believable that he's any kind of measured drugs cheat; much more likely, knowing the man as a bit of an absent-minded professor, it's a screw-up. But the fact remains that the rules were broken, and when you do that, there's normally a tab to pick up somewhere. It's hard for the average sports fan to take in—a cheat's a cheat, they say from behind their newspapers—but there's obviously far greater complexity involved than I would like to sort out.

This might be as good a time as any to give you a quick look inside the world of the professional cyclist and drug testing.

The first thing to remember is that you have to give the doping inspectors an incredibly detailed itinerary of where you're going to be at any time. No quick changes of plan. No riding to your cousin's for a game of PS4 instead of the four-hour recovery ride because it's started to rain. No dropping in at the hospital to see a friend who is ill. You stick to the itinerary, or you have a bloody good reason for not doing so, and you tell somebody in advance. It's no wonder people make mistakes, and we shouldn't dismiss everybody who makes an error as a cheat. We have to accept that it's as crucial a part of your job as riding up hills, doing sponsors' events, or training properly.

Amid the confusion of our busy weeks, we have to give a one-hour window each day when we absolutely must be at home, or wherever counts as our base if we're away. I say 6:00–7:00 a.m. or 7:00–8:00 a.m., knowing that I'll be available anyway. OK, if you were hoping to sleep in and they knock on the door at 6:00 a.m., it's a bit of a pain, but it's a minuscule price to pay to safeguard the integrity of the sport and our own reputation. If they call outside of that window but during a day that we have listed as being at home, we have one hour's grace to present ourselves. The only time I really struggle with the process is when they call at 6:00 a.m. during a stage race like the Tour de France, where sleep is hard to come by at the best of times and rest is everything.

If you're a stage winner, a jersey holder, or the leader of a UCI category, you will be tested at each and every race. Over the season, I will literally give hundreds of samples, all of which will be tested as if they are the one and only proof of innocence and guilt. With the race controls, the home controls, and the large number of random tests outside of the race, I am probably tested about once a week, evened out over the course of the year. And it's absolutely, definitely, unequivocally worth it. In fact, it's better to be tested all the time, as there is little scope for fluctuations in your numbers. There were stories in the past of riders under suspicion because of big discrepancies between tests, but if you're not tested regularly and you go on an intense period of training at altitude, you'd be disappointed if there wasn't a big spike in your figures. The answer is to be tested more, not less.

Let's say you went out with friends on a Saturday night two weeks ago. You had, say, five pints, a kebab on the way home, went to bed at one, got up at eight, felt great, went out for a bike ride. Then last Saturday, you went out with the same guys, had five pints again, another kebab, in bed by one, then woke up with a horrific hangover and had lost the ability to stand, let alone ride a bike. Sound familiar? We can't always predict how our body is going to react to different things on different days. That's why you need to be tested all the time, because you feel inexplicably different some days despite repeating exactly what you've done previously. You don't want that looking like a squiggly line on your blood passport or eyebrows will rise. Test as often as you can, and all patterns will be smoothed out. Unless you're cheating, and then you'll be caught, and bloody good riddance.

———

Moving on . . . leaving aside the tour contenders, the people I spend most time rubbing shoulders with, literally, are the sprinters. Sprinting is one of those disciplines in sport where your character is on show for all to see. For instance, it's not easy to get a handle on what a swimmer might be like, but nobody who has ever seen Zlatan Ibrahimović play football could be left without having formed some sort of opinion about him as a person. Strange, and possibly wildly inaccurate, but true nonetheless.

Let us accept that one needs to have a certain amount of brio to be a sprinter in the first place, so once again I'm not likely to get drawn into telling you what somebody is really like. But I can tell you their characteristics as sprinters.

The fastest in a straight line, all things being equal, for most of my career has been Marcel Kittel. Just in terms of downright speed, he is a difficult opponent. If everything goes right for him, he'll often win. Fortunately for the rest of us, there are many variables to ruin his day and they do.

As he ages, Marcel could do a lot worse than study Andre Greipel. A gentleman who has the respect of everybody else in any race he rides, especially his fellow sprinters, Andre's skills have kept him at the top of the tree when you could reasonably expect his top-end speed to be blunted by the seasons. We're talking tiny amounts to make a big difference here. His longevity is exceptional. He just knows how to do it better than anyone else and is nearly always spot-on with his judgement.

If Kittel has been the fastest guy pound for pound in the last few seasons, the man for the future is undoubtedly Fernando Gaviria. The guy's raw speed is frightening, he's had a superb tutelage at Quick-Step, and he's only 23. Sure, there'll be others to round out his generation, but they'll have to be fast if he's not to be the king of the castle for years to come. You can't help thinking that when it comes to the flatter stages of the Tours de France of the next few seasons, if you finish in front of Gaviria, you'll win.

In out-and-out explosiveness, Mark Cavendish has ruled the roost for so long it's hard to believe he won four stages of the Tour de France way back in 2008. His maximum speed when he hits the front has remained largely unmatched ever since, although the search for his best form has to go a little deeper these days. The way to beat Cav is to recognize that though his top speed is peerless, it's hard for him to hold it over any length of time, meaning that timing is more important to him than to others. Never give up if he is in front of you, but never write him off if he is behind you.

Alexander Kristoff is the opposite to Mark. His jump is nothing to write home about, but his top speed is like a jet fighter cruising at 20,000 feet. Allowed a long lead-out to wind up his gear and given a gap, he will take some catching. He probably doesn't win as many races as he deserves because many riders, myself included, use his high speed as a launchpad for our own designs, but he is a fearsome competitor. If I added up the closest sprints I've been in over the years, Alexander would probably feature in 50 percent of them, including that incredible arm wrestle for the line in Bergen. It shouldn't be forgotten that this is a man with two Monuments to his name, testament to his ability to ride at the front of difficult races and still produce a winning kick when the rest of the sprinters have fallen by the wayside.

That crossover from sprinter to classics rider is a bit of a gulf, and for a few years, I thought I might not make it. The best example of someone who has done this in modern times must be Tom Boonen. On the podium at Roubaix at 21 and a Tour green jersey five years later, it was Tom's style that was the secret of his longevity. He was just sublimely smooth. You couldn't imagine him breaking a bike. He's the reason that Zanatta believed I'd never win Paris–Roubaix: I smash the bike into every cobblestone whereas Tommeke just floated a couple of inches above them like a Japanese monorail train. Three Rondes and four Roubaix wins aren't things that fall into your lap. Tom rode for Quick-Step for pretty much his whole career, which didn't always give him the advantage you might think. They were so strong with so many potential winners that Tom could be the perfect foil for his teammates—remember Niki Terpstra's Roubaix win, when nobody wanted to tow his team leader back up to the front?

The other giant of the classics is indisputably Fabian Cancellara. He had a different route to the top. For a long time, he had a reputation as a short time trial specialist, but he also ended up with seven Monuments on his mantelpiece, like Boonen. Their careers constantly intertwined. In our first clashes, Cancellara wasn't too pleased with me. My first Tour de France stage came about when I used his late attack to mount my own victory bid, and then he found my silly finish-line salute disrespectful. I earned some respect from him eventually, and he wasn't just a gentlemen, but a smart-enough competitor to recognize that rivalries can be good for everybody. As for me, I just loved the way the man rode a bike. Completely in control with rippling core strength, he was often criticized by the cognoscenti for doing too much work in races, allowing others to profit. You know what? So what? So what if he didn't win every race he could have won? He was an entertainer, a showman who raced as hard as he could every day he got on his bike. That's why fans loved him, not just for his undoubtedly fantastic palmarès, but for the style and panache that lit up every race he competed in. I'll never be Fabian Cancellara, but that's the way I want to ride my bike.

Of my current rivals in the peloton, Michal Kwiato has had the career most tied to mine like a pair of laces since day one. We went to the UCI Junior World Championships in Mexico when we were 17—he with Poland, I with Slovakia—only to see Diego Ulissi win the road race. Michal won the time trial in Cape Town the following year, while I won silver in the cyclocross race. He's got such amazing staying power for somebody who looks so reedy. I struggled with distance in the earlier part of my career, but, bearing in mind we're exactly the same age, Michal won the longest one of them all, the UCI World Championships at 24. He'd already seen me off that spring with a great late attack at Strade Bianche that I couldn't match. He's the last guy to wear these lovely rainbow threads before me, and it would be a brave man who would bet against him winning it again someday. You wouldn't get very good odds on it being him versus me for the right to wear them again before our careers are through. He's also the winner of probably the best race I've been involved in, that Milan–San Remo where I stuck it to the bunch on the Poggio but couldn't shift either him or Julian Alaphilippe and Kwiato ran me out in that incredible three-up sprint on the Via Roma. Underestimate this man at your peril. I don't think there's any race where you could declare outright that Michal couldn't win it.

Last but not least is GVA, Greg Van Avermaet, the two of us seemingly inseparable in the bookies' minds. Like me, he's always there. Like me, everybody looks to him. It hasn't been easy for either of us since Fabian Cancellara and Tom Boonen hung up their cleats. Everybody else in the bunch seems to think there are only two wheels worth following, which is patently ridiculous. On paper, you could hardly describe either of us separately or even jointly as dominant, even if he is the Olympic champion, and I'm the world champion. The funny thing about Greg and me is that we have so much in common and are so similar in so many ways. We effectively share the same calendar, the same targets, we both ride aggressively to get into breaks, we can both sprint, we're both threats at the end of long races. Yet we are so different in character. Maybe it's because he's Belgian? There's so much Flemish history piled on those guys' shoulders, so much pressure to be the next Merckx/Van Looy/Schotte/ De Vlaeminck/Museeuw/Boonen. There are always big names around you, riders with specialties, who will be fancied more than others on certain stages. It can either work against you as pressure or for you as camouflage. It used to irritate the hell out of me that if Greg and I are in a group, they treat him like every other rider, yet sit on me like I've got rocket boots on, waiting for me to merely flick a switch and soar into the stratosphere. But, and this might have to do with the retirements of those two titans, I think that presumption is changing, and he's now finding it harder to get away too. He's also an extremely nice man, very straightforward and fair, and always a dangerous opponent. You can't imagine Greg going to a race just to make up the numbers, and that will always make him one of the good guys in my eyes.

AUTUMN

Christina O had turned my year around. All 99 meters of her. Of that I was certain. All I needed to do now was ride my bike, and everything would be right with the world. Sometimes the best plans in the world are the simplest ones. Why so serious?

Sticking to the tried and tested, I headed back to Park City, Utah, for some quality training at altitude and more peace of mind. There's something about the United States that seems to cool my bones whenever the plane touches down. I love the pace of life in the West so much. A couple of weeks riding, eating, and sleeping at 2,200 meters above sea level certainly speeds up the training process, even if the first few days give you legs of lead and a tiny pair of lungs that would struggle to blow up a kid's balloon. By the time my next scheduled races in Canada started to loom up in the diary, I was flying.

I went back to the start line of the Grand Prix of Québec as the reigning champion, feeling good about the day and the coming weeks, since this was where Project Desert had really taken wings a year earlier. It's a good test for the world's in many ways, not just because of its position in the calendar just before the big festival, but it's a circuit, which is always a little different than a point-to-point race. You get a chance to look at the finish a few times, to see where people go hard, the corners that can cause problems, the likely launch points for attacks.

You'll know by now that my philosophy is that no two races are ever the same, and yet the GP Québec 2017 could hardly have been more similar to 2016. As in the previous year's race, Rigoberto Urán tried a long-distance sprint a couple of times in the last few hundred meters, and then there was a mess of lead-out trains getting in each other's way. The trick here is not to panic, but to rely on your speed and be glad that the pace is high enough to make getting swamped unlikely. Sure enough, with about 150 meters to go as they weaved across the road and lead-out men faded and pulled over, a tasty Sagan-shaped gap opened up right in the middle of the road, and it was a straightforward blast to the line from there.

Like 2016, Greg Van Avermaet was next over the line, leading the press to ask me afterward if there would be a repeat in Bergen two weeks later. "There will be a lot more riders than Greg and me in Norway," I told them. A hundred riders, a hundred stories. Or in Bergen, more like two hundred riders and two hundred stories.

It was then pointed out to me that this was my 100th victory as a professional. A different hundred stories. Yes, of course, it's a number to be proud of, but in the moment, any one of those victories was more enjoyable to me than looking at them as a whole. Maybe when I'm a fat old guy trying to persuade Marlon that I used to be somebody once upon a time, I will dig out a silly fact like this, but until then I'll just carry on trying to win every day I race. "I'd rather live to be a hundred years old than win a hundred races," I said to the flashbulbs.

The other Canadian race in Montreal, two days later, didn't deliver number 101, but despite the disappointment people might have expected me to feel, it was a really useful exercise. If I hadn't learned by then that with the UCI rainbow stripes on your back and form in your legs, it's only to be expected that the other riders will follow your every move, then I'd not been paying attention. "Go on then, champ," they might as well be saying, "show us what you've got." I think that's fair enough, and it's never likely to be as bad when you get to the world's, when any number of other riders arrive with the intention of taking the gold medal home with them. Sure, they're going to look to see what you're doing, but they're going to be more inclined to do something themselves, and the higher the number of potential winners, the longer the odds of the favorite, even if you're still the favorite.

So, I ended up having a really hard race in Montreal, and so did the team, closing down all the moves ourselves, being marked immediately when we tried something. The whole BORA-hansgrohe unit, including Juraj, who would be with me in Norway again, had worked really well at Québec, really controlling the front of the bunch when the race got to the business end, and they were flat out again today. When the attacks started coming late on, nobody—and I mean nobody—would help us chase, just following my wheel in the hope that I would bring the move back and they could all counter. I sprinted in just behind Greg and Michael Matthews, the same top three (in a different order) as two days earlier, but this time we were seventh, eighth, and ninth. It was hard, but just what I needed.

I flew back from Canada to Monte Carlo for a few days as I was doing the team time trial in Bergen. The TTT is always at the beginning of the world's festival, giving the riders and teams time to regroup for the elite road race the following weekend. I'd had the best preparation possible for the world's. I had the benefit of two winning experiences under my belt. *Christina O* and Canada had brought me virtually to the start line in the best shape of my career.

And then it all went wrong.

I woke up in Monaco with a fever. Snot and sweat were pouring out of me like rats fleeing a sinking ship. Riders often get sick: We play with fire by asking too much of our bodies. Physically, we sail as close to the wind as we can, pushing ourselves beyond reasonable limits. It's hardly a great surprise when it goes tits up . . . but this wasn't like that. I'd never been in better form. Yet here I was, shivering and sweating under the sheets in the middle of the day while Monte Carlo buzzed outside. It was just one of those good old-fashioned bugs, picked up from a stranger at a race, in a hotel, on a plane . . . Who knows? I just hope whoever gave it to me was suffering like me in his own bed, somewhere else in the world.

Team Peter swung into action, like it always does in times of stress. Giovanni and Gabriele called Ján Valach to let him know that the chances of me being able to ride the TTT were nil—it was the following day!—and that I had to be a doubt to start the road race. The three of them vowed to be philosophical about the situation, but leave the door open until the race had begun without me. They were agreed that any expectation for me to perform in a week's time was to be immediately dialed back.

Me? I spent three days in bed.

That meant that when I got up and pulled back the curtains on a Monte Carlo morning at last, it was Wednesday. The race was on Sunday, 2,500 kilometers away.

I rode that day and the next. On Friday morning I felt pretty good and phoned round the Monaco gang. If I was going to even start on Sunday, we'd have to ride pretty hard today. So it was that Sylwester Szmyd, Oscar Gatto, Moreno Moser, Alex Saramotins, and yours truly headed out into the Alpes Maritimes on a beautiful, bright, autumnal morning on the Mediterranean. I felt OK, and we were all showing off, determined to give each other a good hard kicking. If you've ever driven down that autoroute from France toward Italy, the one that splits the Riviera from the hills, you'll know there are some pretty hefty mountains bearing down on you. Yes, Monaco is a good place for a pro to live for lots of personal reasons, but being able to ride out of your front door straight onto hills like these is a huge part of the attraction. You can lose yourself—mentally and physically—within a few minutes and forget that the densely populated strip of Nice–Antibes–Monaco is just behind and below you.

In our efforts to show off, plunging down one little rocky road three hours in from the coast, Oscar pulled a spectacular locked-out rear wheel drift around a particularly enticing sweeping right-hander. But, as I know too well, showing off can get you into trouble, and so it proved for Oscar. His rear tire was shaved into a huge flat spot, the inner tube poking out through the casing until it gave up the ghost with a resounding rifle crack.

"*Cazzo*, Gatto? What the fuck?"

We all had a laugh and drained our water bottles, taking advantage of the stop to rehydrate. I ripped off a bit of handlebar tape to cover the inside of the hole in his tire—junior mountain bikers learn how to be practical, you know—and re-inflated it with a new tube. Gabriele says that I think I'm Inspector Gadget or something.

On we went into the mountains, no tiny road ignored, no hill left unclimbed. My repair job lasted an hour. Then—bang! Oscar brings us all to a standstill again.

"*Vaffanculo*, Oscar!"

We take another drink, our bottles refilled many times now from roadside taps and springs in the hills. This time, I rip up an empty one and use the curve of the plastic to sit inside what is left of Oscar's shredded tire. Would Inspector Gadget have thought of that? Another spare tube, and we're back in business.

We've been out six hours now, and we're racing back toward the coast, seeing if we can drop anyone. We flash through L'Escarène and blast up the pass that separates it from Peille. It's a tiny road, and as we dart down the other side, there's plenty of gravel on the corners. As we take one bend, there's a little boulder lying right in our path. Sylwester and I skim it, but the third rider isn't so lucky and hits it flush with his front wheel without ever seeing it. No prizes for guessing the victim . . . it's Oscar.

We race to his side, but it looks bad. He went down straight on his face, and there is blood all over the road. Fortunately, there's a phone signal, and his Astana soigneur is immediately on his way up the mountain at speed, but he's still at least 30 minutes away. We clean up Oscar as best we can and sit him down at the side of the road.

After he is escorted straight to the hospital, we continue in a much more quiet and somber mood, but when we get down to the coast, we're met with the excellent news that there is no significant damage, Oscar's helmet bore the worst of the impact, and he's still going to be a handsome bastard when it heals up.

"We've got to celebrate, guys," I suggest, and we head for the pizzeria. Oscar is OK, and we've just conquered the worst that the Alpes Maritimes can throw at us. Maybe I'll be going to Bergen after all.

I get home, and Maroš goes to work on my battered legs for an hour. I slip into bed for a nap, tired but pretty pleased with the day's work.

An hour later I'm crawling out of bed, barely making it to the toilet in time to vomit noisily and exhaustively. Something I ate? To be honest, it looks like everything I ate. Maybe it was the pizza; maybe it was all those bidons of roadside water.

Shit, shit, shit. I'm flying to Bergen tomorrow. The UCI World Championship Road Race starts in 36 hours. Thanks, rainbow jersey. It's been fun, but I guess it's somebody else's turn now. Good-bye from a true friend.

———

It's a chilly, damp morning in Scandinavia a day and a half later. I have lost count of the number of times I've been to the toilet since that ride. No matter what I eat or drink I feel bloated, or empty, or sick.

There are 40 kilometers of road to cover before we hit the main circuit, then 11 laps of 19 kilometers. Juraj is beside me as we reach the circuit and cross the finish line for the first time. "Take a good look," I tell my brother, "I don't think we'll be seeing this line again."

And then I won.

EPILOGUE

Compiegne is a grand little town for somewhere so unheralded. It has wide boulevards, tall flat-faced stone buildings and squares that encourage a passerby, or passing cyclist, to sit for a while, drink in a little of the peace while sipping on a coffee, a cold beer, or maybe a Ricard, if you've finished work.

It might not, in that case, be entirely inappropriate that for one Sunday morning each spring, Compiegne is asked to stand in for Paris. Not for a film set, though I'm sure they could get away with it, but for the start of the world's best known one-day bike race. And nobody anywhere in the history of cycling has ever called l'Enfer du Nord by the name of Compiegne–Roubaix, have they?

Before the days of big buses, the teams used to gather in the central square close to the start line, the likes of Sean and Patxi have told me. Now, the first guys to show up can still squeeze their enormous Volvos and DAFs with blacked-out windows in, but the rest of us stretch out nose to tail along one of those long tree-lined avenues where huge sedate houses are set back a respectful distance from the asphalt. In 2018, the BORA-hansgrohe truck is the very last in the long line of hi-tech buses parked under the trees that are just beginning to leaf. This is not a bad thing for the calm and collected townspeople of Compiegne, nor for the other teams. I'll tell you why.

A year or so back, I was introduced to these amazing Bang & Olufsen speakers that look like satellite dishes. If you go to my house, you'll see them, and in my dad's house, and my brother's . . . they're really cool. Well, this spring we brought a couple along to the races. And though Paris–Roubaix doesn't start in Paris, BORA-hansgrohe are giving the citizens of Paris every chance of hearing the start even though they're 80 kilometers away. The speakers sit outside the door to the bus, instantly turning the springtime avenue sprinkled with birdsong into the darkest, deepest, dirtiest, Bratislava nightclub. There's a huge crowd around our bus, and you can see staff from the other teams craning their necks to look over, part envious, part disapproving. But our fans love it, we love it, I love it. We are here to entertain, we're here to make an impression, but most of all we're here to win. The mood is summed up perfectly by Patxi as DS, when the UCI lanyards arrive to give our bikes the once-over.

"How are you, Mr. Vila?" he is asked.

"Ready," is his one-word response.

As they go about their business, passing their iPads over the S-Works frames in the belief that if any are harboring secret motors, alarm bells will ring, they each blink inadvertently in time with the music. Why so serious, guys?

———

It's been a strange spring, to say the least. I'll give you a quick recap to put this Roubaix in a bit of context.

This year we were trying something different. In a plan devised by Patxi and Sylwester, now respectively my DS and coach as opposed to my coach and friend, we had decided to prioritize the central northern classics of Flanders and Roubaix as the days where I should be reaching my best form. This was a bit of a shift from previous years, and a fantastic illustration of what I was saying about Ralf and Willi at BORA-hansgrohe and the difference between them and Tinkoff. With Oleg, his passion and excitement always meant that he wants to win now, today, every day. Now, Patxi, and before him Sean, also have experience of working with Grand Tour winners like Alberto Contador, Chris Froome, and Bradley Wiggins, where tapering your training for specific races and maintaining your best form in the crucial weeks of the season has proved essential to their success. Patxi and Sylwester wanted to do this with me, arguing that the glut of podium places through the spring was all well and good, but we would always trade a dozen days of being sprayed by somebody else's champagne for a Monument.

And of course, Ralf and Willi said, "Sure, you know best." That's the difference. They didn't just hire Team Peter for our ability to get results; they trust us to know best. That's pretty cool. It's higher risk because BORA-hansgrohe gets less exposure week in, week out, and if I then fail in my targets, it's an overall loss. But, and this was where Patxi and Sylwester were convinced, it's a little bit closer to my dreams of winning the biggest races.

This doesn't mean entirely sacrificing races like Strade Bianche or Milan–San Remo, but it does mean racing them on my way to top form, rather than finding that form first.

Accordingly, Strade Bianche was my first European race in 2018. I came close again at Milan–San Remo, but once again ended up on the wrong end of a quite brilliant race. Vincenzo Nibali held me and some other guys off for a really great victory in San Remo, making him the winner of the two most recent Monuments, with his similarly audacious first place in the Tour of Lombardy at the end of 2017. The man is a great showman, and I take my hat off to him. Is it better to lose a great race than win a boring one? I'm not sure. I will try to win great races in the future so that I don't have to ask myself again.

Almost every race I compete in, I seem to start among the favorites. The retirement of Tom Boonen and Fabian Cancellara hadn't helped me one bit either . . . superb riders like Niki Terpstra and Greg Van Avermaet still don't cast as long a shadow as those guys, and as a result it often feels like Me versus The Rest. I try to take it as a compliment and use it to my advantage, but at my low ebb it can be soul-destroying.

On the plus side, the classics team we had put together at BORA-hansgrohe was the best I've ever been in. Having managed to hook Daniel Oss from BMC, not only did we have another high-powered gun, but it left Greg short of one. Body and Burghardt were both flying and incredibly motivated, and Juraj was riding better than at any time in his career.

So we went to Gent–Wevelgem, and I fucking won. You know that I don't swear very often—only in the bunch in Flemish—so maybe that will give you an indication of how much it meant. Burghardt was imperious throughout. Some of the great names have worn that German champion's jersey over the years, and it brings out the best in Marcus. Knowing that he can not only pull the race back together on his own, even with 230 kilometers in the tank, but that if you take your eyes off him he will win, makes him a massive weapon in the BORA-hansgrohe armory. I doubt the group would have reached the finish intact without his power or the fear he sowed in the others. Then my nose for sniffing out the best line in the sprint showed itself to be intact.

I didn't think I was at my fastest yet, but I was winning long races and outsprinting quick guys like Viviani and Démare to win them. Three times Gent–Wevelgem winner. I like threes. A week later at the Tour of Flanders, I felt I did everything I could. We talked earlier about Tom Boonen's long shadow at Quick-Step, and his retirement really has loosened the reins on his former teammates. Now they all felt that they could win. Daniel Oss put in his first immense performance for BORA-hansgrohe when I asked him to "make it hard" (remind me never to say that to him at a training camp), but with Niki Terpstra, Philippe Gilbert, and Zdeněk Štybar all cruising for Quick-Step, his effort helped all the big names, not just me. Terpstra used an attack by Nibali—that guy!—as a springboard and soloed away. I tried my usual trick of carrying my speed around that dead corner at the bottom of the Paterberg then going up it like my back wheel was on fire and burning my arse. It worked to a certain degree: I went clear of the others, but Terpstra was too far gone and flying. Such is life. I felt that at least I'd tried, and I hadn't died wondering. Organizing a chase with Greg, Nibali, and the others was always going to be difficult with those blue Quick-Step jerseys sitting on us, and they would have been freshest at the death, even if we had reeled in their Dutchman. I tried on my own, but it wasn't to be. I faded back to the chasers, and Terpstra took a great Monument victory.

So. Here we were. Compiegne. The pivotal moment of my spring. Since Flanders last weekend, I'd come as close as I'd been all spring to being happy. That's maybe not the right word for it, but making that switch of focus to Belgium and caning the roads, while enjoying riding with friends, was a feeling I'd lost, and it would make do instead of happiness for the time being.

All the talk in the week before Roubaix was about how it was going to be wet.

I don't think I've ever ridden a really wet Paris–Roubaix, the sort of races animals like Giovanni will tell you are for real bike riders. I've seen videos: Andrei Tchmil and Franco Ballerini in the 1990s, or Johan Museeuw's epoch-defining solo win in the last wet edition, 16 years ago now. That was the day Tom Boonen announced himself too. His whole brilliant career had passed by since that epic day without it ever chucking it down in Le Nord on the second Sunday in April.

There was a big groundswell of fans begging the clouds to burst. #prayforrain was trending on Twitter. And on those days between De Ronde and l'Enfer du Nord, it did rain. We had a hoot scouting the route, splashing the hell out of each other, care-fully guiding teammates into the deepest troughs and ugliest puddles just for the hell of it, with laughs and challenges handed out over coffees on the way. I had new kit, and I was going to test it to within an inch of its life. Not bothered about bikes? Skip this next bit ...

Specialized makes three main road bikes. There's the Venge, the aero one, popular with the likes of Daniel Oss with his long levers and time trial heritage. I'll use a Venge sometimes, usually when speed is the only consideration. Isn't it always the only consideration, Peto? But no. The Venge is a no-compromise weapon, so it's a harder ride and less versatile than some. We'll use it for, say, a shortish stage of a race on good roads that's likely to finish in a group kick for the line.

For most days on the bike, with corners, climbs, descents, changes of pace, and the need to leave yourself feeling OK to do it all again tomorrow, you need more versatility. My mount of choice is the Tarmac, long the flagship of Specialized's road range and the perfect all-around weapon.

But the third bike is designed with the paying customer in mind, a comfortable long-distance machine that will soak up all sorts of shit and still have you flying at a finish line. What's it called? That's right. The Roubaix.

This is the only day I'll really use this bike. I might ride it at a race like Scheldeprijs to make sure it's working OK, but for me this bike has one job only.

Specialized made two S-Works Roubaix bikes for me just for this race, both in my custom gold and black colors, one with rim brakes and one with discs.

With the move across cycling toward disc brakes and their ability to work better in bad conditions, it makes sense that all Roubaix models available to buy are now fitted with discs. I don't have a problem with discs at all, but the issue in Paris–Roubaix always has been and always will be punctures and mechanicals. I might need to grab a wheel from anywhere to sustain a winning move or avoid being dropped when the pace is high, and the last thing I want to deal with at that moment is compatibility. Basically, with will, elbow grease, and the correct swear word at the right moment, you can slam any old wheel into any old bike . . . but not if it's got a disc brake rotor on it. We were aware that probably 90 percent of the spare wheels out on the parcours were still going to be designed for traditional bikes, and that swung it for us: Stick to the old school.

Patxi and I then decided that electronic gears were not going to be necessary. With the ludicrous pavé of Paris–Roubaix constantly smashing at your bike from below, there is always a chance that a connection somewhere could get jiggled out of place and you lose your gears. Also, it's not like Flanders where gear choice is super-important for bergs like the Koppenberg or the Muur. Really, if it came to it, you could ride Roubaix on a single speed.

———

Finally, we were racing. The tweets of chiffchaffs filled the air, blackbirds warbled, the first swallows of spring skimmed the low grass in the fields. Spectators wearing hats to protect cropped heads from the sun carried huge Eskys of cold beers between them toward the remote secteurs of pavé like Jack and Jill on their way up the hill. A lot more Jacks than Jills, too, it has to be said. The Belgians and Dutch singing impenetrable folk songs, the French blasting grimy Parisian rap from barely portable sound systems, and the Anglos trying to blend in. Wet, it was not. Yes, there were some residual puddles, some that had no doubt been in situ since about October, but it wasn't anything like the #prayforrain gang had hoped for.

My number was 111, which felt good, as the special new skin-suit that Sportful had been developing for me was called the Bomber 111, and now it had that same number pinned to it. They called it 111 to reference each of my world titles, but it's also the number of the Heinkel bomber that caused so much devastation during the Second World War. I hoped to make it through to the outskirts of Lille without getting caught by angry Spitfires.

The early forays in Roubaix aren't quite the same as in other big races, as you still get the frenzied start with a lot of people and teams keen to be involved in the break, but it doesn't calm down afterward. The knowledge that the first real pavé sections begin around Troisvilles after about 100 kilometers means that the race is always going to be fast, whether a break has gone or not. You really can't expect to be held up by a crash or a big split at Troisvilles and still win the race, so it's a supremely hard and tactical couple of hours when your teammates are precious. Five guys did manage to get clear, but the pace was still nervously high behind them, even though there was no great need to reel them in.

The last 10 kilometers up to the Troisvilles secteur is like the last 10 kilometers of a first week Tour de France stage. Quick-Step, Sky, BMC, FDJ, BORA-hansgrohe . . . we're all smashing the pace at the front, and it's line astern all the way back from the first man to last.

Then it's on at last. Slightly downhill, the huge camber of the road leads in the unwary off the crest and into hellish troughs on either side. "Relax, relax, relax," is my mantra, when every logical atom of your being is screaming at you to do exactly the opposite: Don't relax. Tense up. Panic. Stop. Do something!

Dust clouds thicken the air and shorten the field of vision. It's best to have a clear view, but if you've got a clear view, you're either on the front of the race or you've been dropped. Everybody else just has to get on with it. We try to remember our recon rides, but it's impossible to visualize each little trench or hole with any accuracy. With the cobbles smashing at your bike, you force your eyeline up and away from the cobble that your tire is about to hit and try to keep it fixed on the middle distance and bring some semblance of technique and normality. The S-Works Roubaix has dampening in the front end, which hardly turns this into a plush sedan chair ride, but does at least convince you that you may be able to retain your eyeballs within their sockets. This is the first section, sure, but there's the knowledge that this will be a huge hurdle crossed if you can make it through unscathed.

All sorts of noise from behind, and there's clearly been a crash. A big one by the sounds of it. It's hard to hear much on the radio in these moments, but it looks like we're OK as a team. The first thing I hear of consequence is that Greg Van Avermaet is delayed.

Have you ever sat in a jacuzzi on full gas when the bubbles stop and it all settles down? God, I love that moment. That is the moment when you leave a pavé secteur and regain tarmac. It feels like an all-encompassing calm. The horizon goes from a lie detector graph going crazy to a thick, smooth swish of the Sharpie in an instant. But there's another one coming.

Quick-Step is all on the front now. This is their chance to take the game away from BMC. You can't win Roubaix here, but you can lose it in a blink.

This is great for BORA-hansgrohe. I feel OK. Burghardt is cruising, as is Body, as is Oss. We'll have some matches to burn in this race for sure. Right now we're lucky that it's Quick-Step and BMC burning theirs up in a head-to-head, and we're tucked in keeping ours dry.

By the time we hit Saint Python—I'd love to read his biography one day, I think whenever I pass the village sign on a recon ride, but always forget—Tony Martin is showing the value of having a powerful horse on your team by dragging the whole race along on his own. There are more crashes, already plenty of abandons, and reports of ambulances and injuries behind us. We have a BORA-hansgrohe headcount and push on. GVA finally makes contact after a really hard chase neither he nor his team will have enjoyed, but I know from my own experience that sometimes that fury can stoke your fire for later in the race rather than sap your strength.

People often talk of the Forest of Arenberg as the hardest section of all, but also say that it's too far from the finish to make a huge difference to the winner. I don't really agree with either reading to be honest: It's different and ludicrously difficult, but it comes, as secteur 19, after half a dozen wickedly exhausting secteurs that are each quite capable of ending your race at any moment. So the idea of it being calmly strategic disappears immediately. And if you do manage to make a proper split in Arenberg, the second half of the trench is so hard and long that it's a fantastic opportunity to hole your opponents below the waterline, especially with more long and sapping sections following soon after.

Two Mitchelton-Scott riders prove my point by having their race ended in the most painful style shortly before we swing below those huge mine workings that guard the entrance to the forest. Coming here on the recon rides last week reminded me of just what a weird place this is. On any other day, the long flat grove of trees is silent apart from patchy birdsong. It is a proper Hansel and Gretel type of enchanted forest—definitely Brothers Grimm and not Bambi—where the chance of seeing a ghost flitting between trees seems almost likely. The story goes that the great Jean Stablinski, formed of the grit and coal that he and his emigré family had worked with their bare hands to become one of the greatest classic riders of all time, recommended this strange and secret pathway through the trees to the organizers. He had chipped out tunnels below it and ridden his bike above it, like *Stranger Things*.

But today, the crowd is roaring, the hot dogs are sizzling, and the sun is shining. Marcus Burghardt leads us onto the opening cobbles, spiking up to meet us like broken girders growing through the earth, me in third wheel, all of us going faster than bicycles ought to be able to go in such inhospitable terrain. This is it. The race. Come on, Marcus. This is it.

Fifty of us left in the front. Paris–Roubaix is the classic shakedown, bike racing as it was intended.

The five-man break is still away, but Burghardt's massive effort has given me that rare delight of choosing my own path through Arenberg. The crazy speed of the first third is quickly replaced by the horrific drag of the second third, but I can see my long, straight route ahead. The tunnel of noise that has seen this little bit of France likened to a flat Alpe d'Huez in the past has been strangely transformed by only allowing spectators on the right-hand side. Here they scream, eyes popping, just inches from our right ears, while to the left is the lonely desolation of straight tree trunks, where you dare not let your eye stray, lest you lose your concentration and be pitched out of the saddle teeth first, or maybe catch sight of a long-dead relative urging you on.

Daniel Oss is with me, and Philippe Gilbert is going like a train as we fight out of the forest and onto the road. There's about 90 kilometers left, and this is definitely Fast Phil territory. As his former teammate, Daniel knows this well, and we watch him closely, though watching and neutralizing are hardly the same thing in this race. Gilbert and Teunissen from Sunweb steal 20 seconds from us, and it's down to BORA-hansgrohe and BMC to do something about it, hopefully before we hit the next volley of pavé. Teamwork makes less difference on the cobbles, and the variables stack up alarmingly.

There are a bunch of secteurs around the foot of a charming cooling tower set in the middle of nowhere that anybody who has ridden these mad roads will remember. The race is arranged in such a way that you feel that you can never leave the power station behind. Time after time you pass it, you look up a few minutes later, and there it is in front of you again. That day with Alberto chasing Nibali in the Tour de France, Oleg's advice to "Fuck 'em all!" ringing in my ears comes back to me. Gilbert's still up the road. I'm flying, on fantastic form, but we've been here before. One hundred stories. And as Zanatta said, I will never win Paris–Roubaix because I'm too hard on the bike.

Who got that deal of signing Daniel Oss over the line? Give him a bonus. The piston-limbed Italian and I were teammates as youngsters at Cannondale, and now we're back together. He pays back a year's worth of salary by catching Gilbert for the team, for me, for the rest of the race. Well played, Daniel. Seventy kilometers between us and the velodrome.

The front of the race splinters and reforms a bewildering number of times over the coming sections. A bike commentator used to other races has no chance. It's twos and threes from front to back, with people jumping forward and sliding back between them constantly. Imagine a horse race like this! It'd be more like a stampede or a cavalry attack than a race. Štybar, Naesen, Van-marcke, Degenkolb, Rowe, Stannard, Stuyven, Terpstra, Greg, Gilbert, Martin are all here, plus me, Daniel, and Marcus flying the BORA-hansgrohe flag . . . and still three members of the original break hang on a few seconds in front of us. This is the race, right here. Tony Martin attacks and is caught. Daniel attacks and is caught. Niki Terpstra attacks and is caught. Greg launches a really hard one that stretches everybody out . . . and is caught. Now it will calm down. I drift through to the front as Greg drifts back along the line, watching his chasers as they watch him. I take five meters. Ten. Twenty meters. Then I give it everything I have.

As ever in Roubaix, we're taking multiple 90-degree bends through a little hamlet otherwise untroubled by the twentieth century, let alone the twenty-first. The corners as we leave the village allow me to glance back. Marcus rolls gently on the front. Greg, recovering from his effort, sits on his wheel. Behind him, everyone else sits and looks at each other. What are they waiting for? I ask myself. Me to chase myself so they can follow, probably. Suckers.

After five minutes of concerted riding, I catch the three guys that have been away all day. Fair play to them. We've got 50 kilometers to go, so they've been out here for the best part of 200 on their own. I'm not really that familiar with them: There's the Swiss champ Silvan Dillier who I know is no mug, Sven Erik Bystrøm, and a strong Flemish guy from Lotto called Jelle Wallays. To expect a great deal of support from these guys would be unreasonable considering what they've already achieved today. I decide to work as hard as I can, treating it like a lone attack, and accepting some respite from them when they're able. That means a welcome injection of energy that they weren't expecting, so they all dig deep to linger at the front of the action for a little longer.

Bystrøm is cooked from his effort and falls away as the pace rises, but the three of us are all going OK. When I caught them, we were about 20 seconds off the front of the bunch. Now, despite these two guys being out here since virtually first thing this morning, they stay with me through the horribly screwed up long section of utterly useless cobbles at Mons-en-Pévèle, and we eke the gap out to 48 seconds. It's now 4:15 in the afternoon. There are 45 kilometers between us and the famous old velodrome. That's about an hour. Come on, Peter. This is your shot.

I can hear on the radio that the race is splintered behind. Nobody wants to get together to chase, but even if they did, it's hard work at Roubaix where the constant thrust of cobbles and changes of direction make it too much of a free-for-all. Apart from Quick-Step, it didn't appear to me before I'd attacked that there were any other teams with significant numbers either, BORA-hansgrohe being one of the strongest, and now we had Marcus and Daniel able to ride on the other teams' leaders in the hope of being fresh if I were to be caught. AG2R and Lotto also stood to make podium positions at least with my breakaway partners, and who could say what would happen to me in this last hour? They could be sprinting for famous victories. All that helped weigh down their own teams' willingness to join the chase.

We came off the next section of cobbles, and I could immediately feel something was wrong. I looked down. Shit. My stem and handlebars were pointing north-west, and my bike was going north. They were out by about 30 degrees. If they're stuck there and won't budge, then I can factor that in and deal with it. But that's unlikely. What's likely is my stem bolt has shaken loose and the whole assembly has swung left. Come the next secteur, they could do a complete 180, and I'll be somersaulting over them into Napoleonic road and my own ignominious defeat. Shit shit shit. Team car? Forget it. This road is about 2 meters wide, and there are 30 battered cyclists in groups of ones and twos between me and the steering wheel Ján Valach is behind. Neutral service? By the time I stop, get a spare bike with the right pedals and adjust the saddle, Ján will have gone by, let alone, Greg, Terpstra, Gilbert, and anybody else whose bike still works.

Shit shit shit. I can't let anyone know. If word gets back to the chasers, it'll be all the boost they need. If these two realize, they'll either drop me or give up. Neither looks good. But I won't be able to chase, to corner, to stand up, to sprint . . . what to do?

I wonder how loose it is. Maybe I can nudge it straight? Impossible with no way of holding the wheel straight though: I give the

handlebar a smack and everything just jogs. Pointless. Wait . . .
what if I could wedge my wheel up against something? As we pedal
through and off, after my turn, Dillier comes through to lead, and
I drift back to Wallays's wheel. I let my front tire ride close so it
actually overlaps his back wheel on his left. Now, if I were to touch
his wheel unexpectedly in this situation, I would almost certainly
crash, and he would be fortunate not to. But planning it? That
would be different, right? A quick sharp tap, straighten the bars
up, and off we go like nothing had ever happened. Right?

"*Godverdomme!*" yells the Lotto guy in the most useful
time-honored swear word in the Flemish cycling bible.

"Oh, sorry, sorry, lost it for a moment, sorry," I apologize.

He shrugs. It happens. I'm the world champion, so I must
have at least a vague notion of what I'm doing . . . worse things
happen every minute of every race.

It didn't work. I tap through again to the front. We really are
going to be on cobbles again soon. This can't be how I lose Paris–
Roubaix. What about all that shit about making your own luck?
All those tire pressure conversations? Lomba writing me off?

I know what I did wrong. I didn't tap him hard enough, obviously. Two or three quick hard blows. That'll do it. Neither of us
fell off last time, I obviously didn't give it enough welly.

I sidle up behind his Ridley again. Deep breath, Peter. This is
it. One . . . two . . .

Bang! Bang! Bang!

"What the fuck, Sagan? What are you fucking doing?"

"Oh man, sorry, just tired, sorry, it's OK."

There's no friendly shrug this time, just a stream of under-his-breath invective and total confusion. Poor guy; 200 kilometers at the front of the world's biggest one-day bike race, and now some idiot is pranking him. This is a man at the end of his tether.

Worse than that, it didn't work. Shall I get off? Twist it straight? Ask the other two if they happen to be carrying Allen keys and try not to get a Lotto-mitted punch in the face?

At that very moment, my guardian angels appeared alongside me in the BORA-hansgrohe Ford. I could have leaned in and kissed them. The lengthy tarmac stretch had enabled Ján Valach and Enrico Poitchke to rally-drive past the chasers and get up to the front.

"Going good, Peter. Need a drink, some food?" enquired Ján.

"Got a four-millimeter Allen key, Ján?"

Everyone loves a four. It's the one you get free with Ikea furniture. A minute later, and we were back in the game.

Half an hour remaining. Seven cobble sections to go. Greg and Terpstra are slowly closing. Time to burn some more matches. I tear through the Cysoing section, and our lead holds at 50 seconds, but not for Wallays, who can't go with this pace. Poor guy. Humiliated, teased, and dropped. I will apologize.

Dillier is riding amazingly well. I keep expecting him to sit on, but he keeps on coming through and giving me little turns. The best thing about this guy is that he thinks he can win this. And the worst thing about this guy is he thinks he can win this. Do not underestimate this man, Peto. He's on a special day.

I heard somewhere once that Sean Kelly blew what most thought would be the first of many Tour of Flanders wins by confidently leading out the sprint from the small group he had shaped, prepared his victory salute only to see Adrie van der Poel's lanky Dutch nose peek round him and snatch a great win. Kelly's lesson? "It doesn't matter how good a day you're on, always remember there might be somebody else on just as good a day who is cleverer than you." Unbelievably for the most quintessential "Flemish" rider, that was as close as he got to winning that race. I couldn't let Sylvain Dillier be my Adrie van der Poel.

The gap isn't coming down now. It's going out: 1 min 10 secs; 1 min 22 sec; 1 min 25 secs. Just Carrefour de l'Arbre, that horrible, horrible section to go. The chasers will have held back, knowing that's their last 100 percent effort to pull it back. I've tried to, but shit, I'm up here trying to hold them off; I haven't been taking deep breaths and rolling my shoulders in mental preparation. I'm as close to empty as anyone.

My biggest effort. Like a pursuit rider on the track, timing it to not blow up, but not wanting to hold anything back. I come out of the worst section of pavé of the Paris–Roubaix finale to find Sylvain Dillier panting like an overworked greyhound but still clinging on. The race tells us Terpstra, Van Avermaet, Stuyven, and Vanmarcke are a minute behind. It's just us. This really is it now.

With two sections remaining, they peg us back to 46 seconds. Nothing. Dillier is spent as a weapon but still there as companion.

Go deeper, Peter. Think. Think of all those races your dad drove you to all over Europe. Think of Juraj's posters of Ullrich and Pantani. Think of Giovanni having to ride around Lake Tahoe. Think of those Slovakian flags in Doha. Think of Gabriele marshaling the media. Think of Marlon's little hands. Go deeper.

Fifty-one seconds.

Fifty-four seconds.

Fifty-nine seconds.

We're on the long avenue that tracks up the outskirts of Lille into Roubaix. The velodrome is up there on the right. This is it. I've been here before, but not to win it. How is Dillier thinking of winning? It doesn't matter. Just do it right, and you will win, Peter. Do it wrong, and he will win. It's in your hands, not his.

He leads into the velodrome and hugs the top of the track, ducking under the spectator's flags, correctly showing me only one way past. Hold. Hold. We have a lap and a half of the old track to complete. We take the bell still on the outside of the track, not as slow as fixed-wheel cat-and-mouse Olympians, but not racing any more. His neck is permanently clicked left, watching me and the track in front. Two more bends. Hold. Hold. Two hundred and fifty meters. Hold. One more bend. Hold, Peter!

Two hundred meters. One hundred and fifty meters. One hundred meters. Now!

I dart down across the track, and Dillier flicks across to go for my slipstream, but I have left it late enough that there is no time for him to catch and overtake me.

I win Paris–Roubaix.

———

In the midst of life, we are in death. A boy died today. A young Belgian guy called Michael Goolaerts with his whole life ahead of him. On the second cobbled section, back in the early part of the race, his heart went into cardiac arrest, and he crashed, never regaining consciousness.

A hundred stories, but this was Michael's last story when it should have just been one of his first. It could be him here writing about his half a dozen Monuments and UCI rainbow jerseys and us reading it in ten years' time.

It's dangerous what we do. Every day, we risk everything for glory, for money, for our families, for ourselves. And I know it's a word that people tire of hearing me say, but yes, it's a lottery.

A hundred stories. One of us wins Paris–Roubaix; one of us dies at Paris–Roubaix. I wish that he could have ripped that ticket up.

If I have a message, it is this: Live life every day. Not because we are bulletproof, but precisely because we are not. Be kind to each other. Be careful with each other. And live life every day.

LIST OF PHOTOGRAPHS

SECTION ONE

1. Slovak flags in Bergen (Tim De Waele/Corbis via Getty Images); Mid-race in Bergen (Tim De Waele/Getty Images); Bergen sprint (Tim De Waele/Corbis via Getty Images); Bergen podium (Tim De Waele/Getty Images)

2. Young Peter at Liquigas (Yuzuru Sunada); Peter, Basso, and Nibali (Pascal Pavani/AFP/Getty Images); Tour de France 2012 stage 6 win (Tim De Waele/Corbis via Getty Images); Peter's father celebrates (Cycling Weekly); Jersey winners in 2012 (Lionel Bonaventure/AFP/GettyImages)

3. Ján Valach 1999 (Mario Stiehl/Cycling News); Kids Tour 2015 (Peter Sagan Kids Tour); With Žilina children 2015 (Samuel Kubani/AFP/Getty Images)

4. Bobby Julich addressing Tinkoff team (Luca Bettini/BettiniPhoto); In conversation with Bjarne Riis (Tim De Waele/Corbis via Getty Images); Peter and Tinkov in green jersey (Tinkoff/SaxoBank); Tinkov with fists raised 2016 (Luca Bettini/BettiniPhoto)

5. Feltrin, Tinkov, Riis (Luca Bettini/BettiniPhoto); With Contador at Tinkoff (Tinkoff/Valamar Hotels & Resorts); 2016 Tinkoff team (Luca Bettini/BettiniPhoto)

6. Richmond team time trial (Bryn Lennon/Getty Images); Richmond sprint (Tim De Waele/Corbis via Getty Images); Looking back to the pack in Richmond (Tim De Waele/Corbis via Getty Images); UCI World Champion celebration (Luca Bettini/BettiniPhoto)

7. Medal in mouth (Luca Bettini/BettiniPhoto); With Michael Kolář, Juraj, and L'ubomír (Tim De Waele/Corbis via Getty Images); Thrown in the air (Tim De Waele/Corbis via Getty Images); Holding up the Slovak flag (Tim De Waele/Corbis via Getty Images)

8. With Tom Boonen after Gent–Wevelgem (Dirk Waem/AFP/Getty Images); Rainbow socks (LC/Tim De Waele/Corbis via Getty Images); Tour of Flanders home stretch (Tim De Waele/Corbis via Getty Images); Podium with Cancellara (Tim De Waele/Corbis via Getty Images)

SECTION TWO

9. Mountain bike wheelie (Tinkoff/Specialized); Rio press conference (Slovak Olympic Committee); Competing in Olympics 1 (Luca Bettini/ BettiniPhoto); Competing in Olympics 2 (Pascal Guyot/AFP/Getty Images)

10. Doha sign-in (KT/Tim De Waele/Corbis via Getty Images); Celebrating Doha (Karim Jaafar/AFP/Getty Images); Hugging Juraj after Doha (Luca Bettini/BettiniPhoto); Three UCI world champions (Bryn Lennon/ Getty Images)

11. Willi Bruckbauer (Brian Hodes/Veloimages); Ralph Denk (Brian Hodes/ Veloimages); Shower advert (hansgrohe); Second place in Milan–San Remo (Yann Coatsaliou/AFP/Getty Images); Tour of Flanders 2017 crash (Tim De Waele/Corbis via Getty Images); Paris–Roubaix disappointment (Brian Hodes/Veloimages)

12. Young Peter and Juraj 2011 (Tim De Waele/Getty Images); Team Peter riders Tour de France 2018 (Justin Setterfield/Getty Images); Sylwester

Szmyd (Graham Watson); With Maroš (Brian Hodes/Veloimages);
In car with Patxi and Gabriele (Patxi Vila)

13. Giovanni Lombardi in T-Mobile kit (Eric Houdas/WikiCommons);
Giovanni, Peter, and Gabriele (Peter Sagan Fondo); Peter and Gabriele
tattoos (Brian Hodes/Veloimages); With Gabriele raincoat (Jordan
Benjamin-Sutton); Team Peter and team bus (Brian Hodes/Veloimages)

14. 2017 Tour de France team presentation (Tim De Waele/Corbis via
Getty Images); Unclipped! (Simon Gill/Action Plus via Getty Images);
Vittel collision (Chris Graythen/Getty Images)

15. Reviewing the Vittel collision (Brian Hodes/Veloimages); Vittel press
statement (Brian Hodes/Veloimages); *Christina O* (yachtcharterfleet.com);
Cigars on board (Peter Sagan); Missing teeth (Peter Sagan)

16. The Hell of the North (Tim De Waele/Getty Images); Winning in
Roubaix Velodrome (Tim De Waele/Getty Images); Roubaix celebration
with Giovanni (Luca Bettini/Bettini Photos); With cobble (Tim De Waele/
Getty Images)

INDEX